ADVANCE PRAISE FOR
WE ARE SO MUCH MORE

"*The stories of these women leaders across the globe are inspirational and illuminating. Aster realistically showcases the challenges and determination these women possessed to reach the top of their careers. And most importantly, it provides a practical roadmap for organizations to develop their talent pipeline to help women leaders to develop and flourish.*"

—**LORRAINE HARITON,** President and CEO of Catalyst

"*Aster's book (hopefully the first of many)* We Are So Much More *uses powerful storytelling as a guide for women and men aspiring to be leaders in their organizations. The inspiration comes from nineteen remarkable women leaders who transparently share their journeys of sacrifice and compromise but also their lessons learned and successes. Can you succeed in your career without giving up on having a family, personal passion, or time for self-care? Aster says yes and shows you how! This is a book for the global career woman.*"

—**SUBHA V. BARRY,** Chief Executive Officer of Seramount
(Formerly Working Mother Media)

"*Congratulations to Aster Angagaw for this significant book,* We Are So Much More*! The time is now to support women and their choices, careers, communities, and families as never before. The book and the nineteen women leaders' profiles share compelling stories through seven key dimensions of their lives. The focus is on a mix of career and personal happiness. Companies are changing and must. We, as women, build a sisterhood of support.*"

—**EDIE FRASER,** CEO of WBCollaborative (WBC, a collaboration of over forty professional women organizations)

"*A must-read for both men and women! I wish I had read this book when I was an up-and-coming leader; the seven key dimensions are so important and resonate with me. If I had known prior to reading this book how important communities were, the way I approached this aspect of my life would have been so much easier and more rewarding. Thank you, Aster, for your insights on how companies can recognize, facilitate, and support women in all of these seven dimensions.*"

—**KIMBER MADERAZZO,** Chairman of C200

"*Aster Angagaw's book* We Are So Much More *is on point and transcends more than the corporate world. It is a must-read for anyone who aspires to learn from professional women who have continually found success in every aspect of their work-life journey. I applaud Aster for her selfless commitment and passion for courageously sharing these hard-hitting stories with timeless lessons! I will add it to my professional reading collection and recommend it universally!"*

—**GWEN BINGHAM**, retired US Army Lieutenant General (three-star)

WE ARE
SO MUCH
MORE

LIONCREST
PUBLISHING

WE ARE SO MUCH MORE

The Journeys of 19 Powerful Women Across Countries, Class, and Color

ISBN   978-1-5445-2465-8   *Hardcover*

978-1-5445-2463-4   *Paperback*

978-1-5445-2464-1   *Ebook*

THE JOURNEYS OF 19 POWERFUL WOMEN
ACROSS COUNTRIES, CLASS, AND COLOR

WE ARE SO MUCH MORE

INTEGRATING THE
7 DIMENSIONS OF SUCCESS
FOR WOMEN LEADERS TO
THRIVE AT WORK AND IN LIFE

ASTER ANGAGAW

CONTENTS

To Helen

A RECKONING FOR WOMEN

"When you feel tired, look back and see how far you have come. When you feel complacent, look ahead and see how much is left to do."

—MY MOTHER, ETABA

Bongiwe Ntuli, Chief Financial Officer (CFO) and Executive Director of the South Africa-based fashion retailer The Foschini Group, has embraced being single and used the extra time to focus on building her career and thinking positively. Certainly this has made it easier for her to network with male colleagues and in most instances break into the inner sanctum of the boys' club. As she grows older and reflects on her professional and financial success, she is happy with her accomplishments but regrets what she didn't do. "I have had a full life," Bongiwe says. "However, if I had been more realistic and more patient, I could have had a fuller life."

Subha Barry was once a top wealth manager at Merrill Lynch & Co. When some prospective clients wanted to switch to "an advisor from the United States" after meeting with the Indian-born

1

woman for the first time, Subha realized that living in the United States would require overcoming systemic discrimination. As she moved up the ladder at Merrill Lynch and other companies and began raising a family, Subha worked so hard to prove herself on the job, while ensuring that everything at home was perfect, that she often slept only three to four hours a night. She often wonders if this lack of sleep made it harder for her to fight off multiple bouts of cancer—first Hodgkin's lymphoma and then breast cancer.

Raja Al Mazrouei, Executive Vice President of FinTech Hive, part of the Dubai International Financial Centre, has spent her life transcending the expectations of her family and her culture. Born in the United Arab Emirates (UAE), into a culture of arranged marriage, Raja overruled tradition and picked her own husband. She is also the only woman in her family to pursue a career. While she is justifiably proud of her accomplishments, she has told me she feels something is missing. "I try to be so many things: mother, daughter, spouse, leader," she said. "And I lose sight of myself."

I've heard many stories like these from women who've made it to the top ranks of business and industry—in places such as South Africa, India, UAE, China, Malaysia, the Philippines, France, the United Kingdom, Brazil, and the United States. They resonate with my own experiences as a woman of color. I was lucky to have a family that raised me to be confident, ambitious, and hardworking, and to have many great mentors and sponsors, both male and female.

I have experienced overt prejudice at work from time to time, which I often ignored. But the higher I moved up the ladder, the more of a target I became. I encountered subtle and not-so-subtle comments questioning how I got my position and whether I deserved it. When I confronted such commenters head-on, they became passive-aggressive and worked behind my back to make my life more difficult. While I eventually learned to deal with this, I didn't always handle it very well, and as a result my relationships, sleep, and overall health suffered at times.

Sadly, this is common in the backstories of high-achieving women in business, especially those of women of color. This is why our ranks are still far too small: while a higher percentage of women than men graduate from college, and while women start careers at an impressive rate, our numbers dwindle higher up the ladder. And we don't make it to the top without doing battle along the way—against persistent bias on the job and unrealistic expectations for managing our relationships and households off the job. We are forced into compartmentalizing our work and home lives, and into making agonizing choices, yet we are judged and unsupported whatever the choice we make.

THE PAUCITY OF WOMEN AT THE TOP OF BIG COMPANIES

Women who strive to make it to the highest level of a company, the so-called "C-suite," still must overcome too many obstacles on the way up and sacrifice too much of themselves to get there— at the cost of their relationships, their personal growth, their interests, and even their health. The problem is most acute for women of color because our barriers to the top are even greater. As a result, we are underrepresented.

For sixty-six years, only one Black woman, Xerox Chief Ursula Burns, held the top role at a Fortune 500 company. Things began to change in early 2021, when TIAA named Thasunda Brown Duckett as its next CEO, and Walgreens chose former Starbucks COO Rosalind Brewer to lead the company. These are breakthroughs, but we still have far to go.

In 2020, only forty-one female CEOs were leading Fortune 500 companies in the United States.[1] That is just 8 percent, and only three were women of color—Joey Wat of Yum China, Lisa Su of Advanced Micro Devices, and Sonia Syngal of Gap Inc.—and not one of them was a Black woman.[2] Women occupy a meager 18.5 percent of top executive positions in the Russell 3000, while 13.4 percent of Russell 3000 companies have no women on their boards.[3] And according to Catalyst, the global nonprofit that tracks how well workplaces work for women, the number of women in the C-suite remains minuscule—only 27 percent in S&P 500 companies, with only 6 percent of *those* serving as CEOs. Only 4.7 percent of executive or senior-level positions at S&P 500 companies are occupied by women of color.[4]

1 Marguerite Ward, "There are now more women CEOs of Fortune 500 companies than ever before, but the numbers are still distressingly low," Business Insider, November 30, 2020, https://www.businessinsider.com/womenfortune-500-ceos-reaches-new-high-2020-11.

2 Alisha Ebrahimji, "Female Fortune 500 CEOs reach an all-time high, but it's still a small percentage," CNN, May 20, 2020, https://www.cnn.com/2020/05/20/us/fortune-500-women-ceos-trnd/index.html#:~:text=Only%20three%20of%20this%20year's,-CEO%20turned%20around%20her%20company.

3 Matteo Tonello, "Corporate Board Practices in the Russell 3000 and S&P 500: 2020 Edition," The Conference Board, Fall 2020, https://conferenceboard.esgauge.org/boardpractices.

4 "Pyramid: Women in S&P 500 Companies," Catalyst, January 14, 2020, https://www.catalyst.org/research/women-in-sp-500-companies.

Why are so few of us leading the biggest corporations in the world when so many of us are more than capable? What kind of political maneuvering and personal sacrifice does it take to get there? And when we do make it, what is it like to be the only woman, and the only woman of color, at the table? We don't have a lot of women at the top who can show us the way or talk frankly to us about the price they paid in their personal lives.

In this book, they do share their experiences. And, based on my personal history and the insights from these remarkable colleagues and friends, here is what I believe:

> *To grow into a leadership role without burning out, a woman must make* **thoughtful choices** *that nurture and integrate seven dimensions of her life: not just* **career**, *but also* **community, play, growth, self-care, money**, *and most importantly,* **purpose**.

In the following chapters of this book, we will explore each of these seven dimensions, why they are important, and what challenges we face in incorporating them into our busy lives. Also included are the stories of women executives and how they worked to nurture each dimension.

WE ARE SO MUCH MORE: ROLE MODELS

In these pages, you will meet nineteen of the most accomplished women leaders I know—colleagues and friends, all corporate leaders, many of them women of color. In Chapters 1 through 7, you will hear the stories of the choices that contributed to these women becoming not only accomplished leaders, but also happier human beings. You will also hear about the setbacks, regrets, and disappointments they faced along the way. Chapter 8 will explore integrating the seven dimensions into our lives, and finally, Chapter 9 will make the case for why loved ones, supervisors, and work cultures must support the "whole" woman.

My prime inspiration—and the reason this book exists—is my mother Zeritu Chernet, who we called Etaba. Like many women of today, Etaba was a wife, a mother, and an entrepreneur—but she was so much more. Her quotes lead off every chapter and her stories and advice are sprinkled throughout the book. She was a remarkable person of great industry and purpose who, despite enduring major hardships, found joy in life and passed it on to others. She showed me that despite my need to make an impact in the business world, **I could be and do so much more**.

I was born into a huge family. I'm the seventh of ten children, a daughter whose birth was sandwiched between three older brothers and three younger brothers. While we were raised in the city, my parents owned a small dairy farm that my father, Angagaw Haile, had founded near our home, so that we would have everything we needed. But during the 1974 Ethiopian revolution following the overthrow of Emperor Haile Selassie, my father, a colonel from the Emperor's Imperial Bodyguard, was sent to jail as a political prisoner. I was in elementary school, and I remember returning home with one of my brothers one day when a neighbor asked if we had been there when they took our father. We didn't know what he was talking about. Back at home, we were stunned to realize our father was gone, and Etaba was on her own to raise us.

That small dairy farm my father set up for us helped our family tremendously because once he became imprisoned, we no longer had a source of income. Imagine: one day we had everything; the next, nothing. Our bank accounts were frozen. All our rental properties, land, retirement income, and investments were gone. All we had was our home and our dairy farm. I watched as Etaba transformed our source of sustenance into a lucrative-enough business that she was able to support us all—thanks to our cows. She suddenly found herself both the head of a household raising a large family and a businesswoman working solo.

Long after Etaba's death in 2001, her example and her teachings have guided me in navigating numerous treacherous roadblocks in my professional and personal lives.

Her life was led by her circumstances. But that didn't mean the choices she made weren't thoughtful or deliberate. She still found time to nurture her children and her friendships, to encourage good values, and to enjoy large gatherings of family and friends at our home. Yet I believe that if Etaba had been given the opportunities my siblings and I were eventually able to seize (in no small part because of her), she would have found her life even more fulfilling. She could have had a more intellectually engaging and rewarding career path, with more time for self-care and everything else she needed. But Etaba was never given the independence to choose her own destiny, without the confines of her culture or the demands of a large family.

I find inspiration in the examples Etaba set. I've been thinking about her a lot lately, about the ways she's shaped me into the business leader I am today, and especially as I've been writing this book. Where I once thought of her life only as constricted by circumstances forced on her, I have come to realize (in writing this book) that she was actually quite deliberate in how she responded to those circumstances, and that made all the difference. Her life story could have justifiably become a tale of woe: her husband and assets were taken away, she was forced to launch and run a business and run a household alone, and without enough resources to comfortably get by. But she made her life story triumphant.

We *all* must be deliberate in everything we do. As I discovered through becoming a partner and spouse, a parent, and a business leader, balance in life is important and can't be left to chance. To this day, twenty years after Etaba's death on September 13, 2001, her guidance is still my North Star. Whether she realized it or not, she was my best mentor. At various points in this book, I will pass along her wisdom, which endures even given how much the world has changed since she died.

THE PANDEMIC'S PUNISHING IMPACT ON WOMEN'S CAREERS

In 2021, the coronavirus pandemic is exacerbating the difficulties women face in the workplace. Research by McKinsey & Company shows that women accounted for 54 percent of pandemic-related job losses globally, even though they make up only 39 percent of the workforce.[5] And those who are still

---

5 Anu Madgavkar, Olivia White, Mekala Krishnan, Deepa Mahajan, and Xavier Azcue, "COVID-19 and gender equality: Countering the regressive effects," McKinsey & Company, July 15, 2020, https://www.mckinsey.com/featured-insights/future-of-work/covid-19-and-gender-equality-countering-the-regressive-effects.

employed are burdened with the lion's share of family responsibilities. More than three times as many women as men are doing most of the childcare and housework. It should be no surprise that millions of women are thinking about taking leaves of absence or resigning from their jobs altogether.

This is a huge problem in an era when many are calling for more diverse C-suites at companies and organizations and when a stronger role for women and people of color is necessary as an antidote to social injustice and as a proven source of tremendous competitive advantage. A 2020 report by Catalyst points out that women around the world control or share 89 percent of the household purchasing decisions, compared to 41 percent of men.[6] People of color, who will make up half the US population by 2045, accounted for $3.9 *trillion* in buying power in 2019, according to the University of Georgia.[7] And a 2019 McKinsey report links diverse executive teams with improved performance: companies in the top quartile for diverse executives were 25 percent more likely to have above average profitability than those in the lowest quartile.[8] Companies won't reap these benefits and connect deeply with an increasingly diverse consumer base without making profound changes that go far beyond the diversity and inclusion programs now in place.

---

6   "Buying Power," Catalyst, April 27, 2020, https://www.catalyst.org/research/buying-power.

7   Matt Weeks, "Minority markets see economic growth," University of Georgia, March 21, 2019, https://news.uga.edu/multicultural-economy.

8   Sundiatu Dixon-Fyle, Kevin Dolan, Vivian Hunt, and Sara Prince, "Diversity wins: How inclusion matters," McKinsey & Company, May 19, 2020, https://www.mckinsey.com/featured-insights/diversity-and-inclusion/diversity-wins-how-inclusion-matters.

The pandemic has worsened the challenges for women who aspire to be organizational leaders. But it didn't create those challenges from scratch. If the following challenges feel familiar and personal, this book is for you:

- **We are underpaid**. Due to pay inequities and the choices women must make between their professional and personal lives, our earnings lag at every stage of our careers. And among the ten occupations where we've lost the most in pay, according to the American Association of University Women, are chief executives, financial managers, accountants and auditors, marketing and sales managers, physicians and surgeons, and medical and health-services managers.[9]

- **We are unfulfilled**. Many women who have reached the top have found it lonely and unfulfilling. Those of us who have devoted our entire lives to realizing our ambitions still may be deeply unsatisfied with our lives. And, the pursuit of our ambitions has come with sacrifices, uncomfortable encounters, and a compartmentalized existence that our male counterparts not only don't experience but also aren't aware of.

- **Women of color, who must fight systemic racial discrimination, as well as sexism, are suffering the most**. According to a study published by the Harvard Law

---

9 "The Simple Truth About the Gender Pay Gap," American Association of University Women, 2018. Updated 2020, https://www.aauw.org/resources/research/simple-truth/#:~:text=Women%20working%20full%20time%20in,debt%20in%20the%20United%20States.

School Forum on Corporate Governance and Financial Regulation, the scarcity of female CEOs correlates with who else occupies the C-suite (the COOs, the CFOs, heads of sales, for example), because these other executives are most often the top contenders for the CEO position.[10] Women, and especially women of color, are simply not being cultivated for those jobs.

- **We overcompensate.** Our response to these inequities is to work extra hard, at great personal cost. Though it's hardly breaking news that women carry more of a burden than men and have had to work twice as hard to get to where we are—and for women of color, three times as hard—it remains an ongoing subject of discussion among us because so little has changed.

- **We are stretched too thin.** Many women are also responsible for caring for others: children, spouses, aging parents, or other family members. Typically, we are expected to take care of housework, raise our children, and tend to family matters. While some of us can afford to hire help, even then it's often up to us to arrange it and delegate tasks. This affects the decisions we make about the career paths we choose—and opt out of. Many of us pass up career opportunities because there is only so much we can take on. Studies have shown that women, more so than men, seek jobs that are compatible with

---

10 Subodh Mishra, "Women in the C-Suite: The Next Frontier in Gender Diversity," Harvard Law School Forum on Corporate Governance, August 13, 2018, https:// corpgov.law.harvard.edu/2018/08/13/women-in-the-c-suite-the-next-frontier-in-gender-diversity.

their domestic lives, specifically child-rearing. They want full- and part-time positions that allow some flexibility, like working from home one or two days a week, or even job-sharing.

- **Our physical and mental health suffers**. This struggle, this role-switching, and this balancing act take their toll—in salary inequities and (especially for women of color) in an "emotional tax," according to a Catalyst report based on survey results of nearly 1,600 US professionals working in business and the nonprofit, education, and government sectors.[11] "Women of color, who often feel undervalued and subject to bias, are constantly 'on guard' because of their gender, race, or ethnicity," reported the Network of Executive Women (NEW). Dnika J. Travis, Vice President of Research at Catalyst, told NEW, "Over time, these daily battles take a heavy toll...creating a damaging link between health and the workplace." Because women of color anticipate and experience bias and endure pay inequities, among other injustices, we frequently leave companies, even as most of us seek leadership positions. That said, according to the Catalyst report, 90 percent of us relish the intellectual stimulation and challenges that come with our jobs, and yearn to thrive and rise within our companies, not leave them.

---

11 Dnika J. Travis and Jennifer Thorpe-Moscon, "Day-to-Day Experiences of Emotional Tax Among Women and Men of Color in the Workplace," Catalyst, February 15, 2018, https://www.catalyst.org/research/day-to-day-experiences-of-emotional-tax-among-women-and-men-of-color-in-the-workplace/.

So, how can we get our share of opportunities in the workplace and also share the burden at home? How can we lean on our loved ones and bring them in to participate in management of the household? Many of us are very good at taking on so much, and we take pride in trying to do it all. But should this really be our end goal? I think not.

WE MUST CHOOSE TO LIVE A FULFILLING LIFE

Over the past few years, I've opened a dialogue about living a fulfilling life with numerous Black, Brown, and white women in the C-suite, from New York City to South Africa, India to Ohio. They hail from an array of cultural and class backgrounds and industries. In these pages, they will share their journeys from childhood to their ascension up the corporate ladder and explain how they manage their lives inside and outside the office.

Here is what I've learned from my experiences and theirs: navigating the seven dimensions starts with uncovering your values—that is, the things in life you cherish most. This process may take time. Once you've identified your values, you then need to examine whether you are living according to them.

Since Etaba died, I have thought a lot about not only how best to honor her memory, but also how her life enabled me—a global business executive, wife, mother, sister, daughter, and friend—to lead a meaningful, fulfilling, thoughtful life.

The ideas of work-life balance and work-family balance don't account for the totality of our lives. I am convinced that the seven dimensions, which I discovered only after much time and soul-searching, can give women a 360-degree view of our lives and how we want to lead them. This book will discuss all seven dimensions in detail, examine the barriers we may face in achieving them, and offer lessons on how to navigate them from women who've made the journey.

Which dimension we are focused on changes based on where we are in life. Taking stock—being aware of where we're thriving and where we need to improve—is key to making thoughtful choices and leading an intentional life. How can we thrive at work when we are not taking care of ourselves, when we are not growing, or when we feel disconnected from our community, our family, our friends, and the rest of the world?

As I spoke with other women in the C-suite, many of whom I met either through the Advanced Management Program at Harvard Business School or through my longtime employer, Sodexo, we shared our stories. We each took stock of how integral the seven dimensions are to our life satisfaction and our sense of success. And we discussed how we'd like to feel even more intentional and fulfilled in our lives inside and outside the office.

THE HARD WORK IN LIVING MORE INTENTIONALLY

I tend to be very achievement-oriented. I can easily forget to stop and savor all the great things around me. Living intentionally requires that I remember to do this every day. I realize I can't always slow down enough to be truly present. But when I remember to do so, it's incredible. It's important for me to stop and appreciate the value of what I have, rather than feeling pain over what I don't.

In subsequent chapters, you'll meet not only Etaba but also women who have reached financial or career milestones and maintained a real sense of achievement and fulfillment according to values and goals set not by others, but by themselves. What emerges as the key to success is the way we have integrated, or worked toward integrating, the seven dimensions that keep us engaged with the world at large and not overly focused on work to the exclusion of everything else.

I have used these dimensions as the organizing principle of this book and show how they have shaped our worldviews and expanded our minds. I explain how they allow us to assess ourselves and our definitions of success, evolve our creative processes, and ultimately achieve a sense of fulfillment.

This is not a traditional self-help book; I don't recommend any one path to find balance. In fact, this book illustrates that there are many paths, and that even the most successful women do not necessarily feel they have found complete balance. Life means constantly being in a state of flux. Often just when we feel we have gotten our bearings, the inevitable changes that come with working and being in relationships with friends and family members have us reevaluating and rebuilding our lives. Throughout this book, you will see how other women navigate these challenges and recalibrate their priorities when necessary.

If you are a young woman starting out in your profession, these stories will provide a perspective on how careers develop and how very accomplished and trailblazing women responded to adverse circumstances. If you are a seasoned professional, you may find in this book a sense of kinship you have not found elsewhere, especially if you often have been the only woman, or the only woman of color, at the table.

And if you are a man of any age, thank you so much for picking up this book. It shows you care deeply for the women around you, and that you are interested in understanding a vantage point that has often been overlooked and underappreciated. I hope the stories collected here help you better understand the obstacles your sisters, daughters, coworkers, and partners face and inspire you to be an ally and an agent for good. Society is better for everyone when women can succeed.

For many of us, the definition of success has less to do with financial gains than with an overall sense of achieving our goals and overcoming barriers. And so the women included in this book have considered such questions as: How present am I in my relationships with family and friends? Do I take the time to care for myself, physically and emotionally? What makes me most proud? How do I find spiritual fulfillment? Cultural enlightenment? What do I do for fun? Does my financial success contribute to my sense of worth, or am I able to savor my achievements independently from what I'm paid? Can I take the time and energy to mentor others, or make other contributions to the world?

Of course, it sounds like a tall order to be able to integrate all these dimensions into our already busy lives. But as you will see throughout this book, the dimensions can naturally overlap. For example, spending time with family and friends can also offer opportunities for cultural outings or recreation that nurture our need for growth and play. Spiritual exploration, be it with a religious congregation or through weekly meditation, can not only nurture our sense of purpose, but also of mind, body, and community.

As we consider which relationships, decisions, and pursuits add up to a fulfilling life, we reflect on our values, and how we all see our lives in the aggregate. In this book, I recount my own journey—from my childhood in Addis Ababa to my education and early career in the United States—and the women featured here (who are from all over the world) reflect on theirs. Although each of us has faced very different cultural, economic, and geopolitical challenges; entered very different corporate environments; and experienced varying levels of support from family and colleagues, we share the drive and determination to be the best leaders we can.

We also share the struggle to be heard, seen, and respected by our male peers who may harbor conscious and unconscious biases. We navigate our own individual battles to define what balance—or integration—and success means for each of us. We prioritize working and living with intention.

I take to heart the lessons I learned both directly from my mother's words and through watching her tend to me and my nine siblings while my father was in political prison. A businesswoman to her core, Etaba didn't get to choose the way she led her life. She wasn't college educated because higher education wasn't available to anyone in Ethiopia at the time. She gave up everything to raise us, and she stepped it up when my father was taken from us. But Etaba was extremely organized: she ran the household and our family's dairy farm as smoothly as the best-run business, while seamlessly finding a way to give each of her children individualized attention *and* carve out time for herself.

Etaba's children had such special relationships with her. After she died, each of us said to the other, "I am sorry to tell you this, I didn't want to hurt your feelings, but I was her favorite, I had a special connection with her." Etaba had a way of ensuring that I knew she saw and heard me by giving me silent acknowledgement of a job well done. Or, if I'd fallen short, she would let me know that I could have put forth a better effort without making me feel reprimanded. I believed that connection I had with Etaba was unique to me and not shared among my siblings.

Etaba's rare ability to make each individual feel special and valued still holds me in awe as a business leader and as a parent. I often think about how I can do this in my own relationships at work and in my personal life. I often fall short of making my daughter, my husband, or others feel special as I go through life multitasking and thinking about the next thing on my agenda. Even when I focus on being present, it does not always come across as naturally as it did for Etaba.

To me, it's about connecting to my soul so that I can appreciate everything. What we focus on becomes our destiny. My hope for every reader of this book is that you will look at these dimensions as potential sources of joy and ask yourself: What do I have in common with these women? Which of these things have I not attended to in my life? What else could I do for myself? The space between where you are and what you become introspective about, while reading this book, is the area where you can grow.

You may ask: How do I pinpoint my intentions and decide what they should be? And how do my choices affect my achievements in work and at home? By the time you have finished reading, I believe you will have multiple answers to these questions.

THE WOMEN YOU WILL READ ABOUT

This book would not have been possible without the stories of these exceptional women from around the world, who have generously shared their personal and professional experiences.

AZALINA ADHAM, Former Chief Operating Officer, Bursa Malaysia

Azalina gained confidence from the Catholic nuns at her all-girls schools in Malaysia and later had the benefit of a Purdue University education and a supportive husband. However, this did not shield her from tough decisions about balancing motherhood with a demanding career at the male-dominated Malaysia stock exchange. Azalina has prevailed, working her way into the C-suite of that organization, which is no small feat.

SUBHA BARRY,
CEO, Working Mother Media

Subha is not only an accomplished professional but also a "change agent"—a six-time cancer survivor, a philanthropist, a mother, and a mentor. She fearlessly railed against the norms and expectations of her traditional Indian family by befriending lepers as a young girl, then studying at an American university (Rice University) and marrying an American man. In her twenty-plus years at Merrill Lynch & Co., Subha was often underestimated because she looked and sounded foreign. Yet she established herself as one of the company's top advisors and became Global Head of Diversity and Inclusion. Her first cancer scare, when her son was just eighteen months old, forced her to reevaluate her life and make bold, new choices.

FLAVIA BITTENCOURT,
General Manager,
Adidas in Brazil

Flavia chose to pursue both a vibrant career and motherhood at an early age, with little family encouragement. After her first marriage ended, she was a single mother for several years. Her children were enthusiastic about her work and she shared its rewards with them, while she built careers in telecommunications and private equity and then at retail brands like Sephora and Adidas. Her story offers excellent insights on balancing a demanding career with a rich family life, even without a strong support system.

MARIA BOULDEN,
Vice President and Executive Partner, Gartner Sales Practice

Maria grew up in suburban Philadelphia, raised by loving Depression-era parents in a happy, middle-class family in an idyllic neighborhood—surrounded by boys. At a very early age, she learned how to respond to sexist comments that began "girls don't..." by proving them wrong. Maria graduated summa cum laude from Drexel University with a bachelor's degree in chemical engineering. She joined DuPont and held roles in research and development, manufacturing, and technology, before graduating to commercial roles and ultimately becoming Global Sales Director for the Safety & Construction platform. She is now Vice President and Executive Partner for the Gartner Sales Practice.

KAREN BROWN,
Founder and Managing Director, Bridge Arrow

Self-discovery, a thirst for continuous learning, and a zest for life are the hallmarks of Karen's individuality. Born and raised in Jamaica, Karen explored many paths in her lifetime with one central goal: to solve problems in order to help people live better lives. Today, she runs a management consulting firm that works with companies around the world on diversity and inclusion. Prior to that, Karen held top D&I jobs at the global law firm Baker McKenzie, healthcare supplier Baxter, aerospace equipment-maker Rockwell Collins, and services giant Sodexo.

LORNA DONATONE,
Former CEO Of Geographic Regions, Sodexo

Lorna's upbringing was not without challenges. The daughter of a former Nebraska governor, she admits to making some bad choices as a teen. But Lorna decided early on that discipline would help her achieve her goals. Eventually, she earned accounting and MBA degrees (from Tulane University and Texas Christian University, respectively). Lorna changed careers several times: from auditing to becoming a top financial executive at an airline to an information technology executive post, then to CFO and president roles at a cruise line, and eventually to CEO of Geographic Regions for Sodexo. With help from a supportive husband, Lorna nurtured her family while juggling major career shifts.

TRACEY GRAY-WALKER,
CEO, American Veterinary Medical Association (AVMA) Trusts

Tracey's journey was filled with ups and downs. Despite an unconventional childhood, she exhibited an impressive sense of self-possession and resourcefulness from a very young age. A loving grandmother raised and encouraged her, and a reading program sponsored by Bell Laboratories and AT&T introduced her to a tutor, books, and the immense possibilities beyond her neighborhood. Tracey's choices have helped her rise in her career while managing her family and her passions. Over twenty years, she advanced from a financial manager to Senior Vice President and Managing Director at AXA US, a large insurance company.

Today, Tracey is CEO of an insurance trust focused on serving more than 95,000 members. She is also the mother of a differently abled adult son. Tracey is currently building a nonprofit designed to create housing for differently abled adults.

LORI JOHNSTON,
Executive Vice President and Chief Human Resources Officer, Amgen

Lori grew up poor and under the limited worldview of her loving, religious family. She made it to the C-suite in human resources at Celanese and Amgen. She was an executive at Dell Inc., the Michael and Susan Dell Foundation, Celanese, and Amgen. Her resilience, ability to pivot, and willingness to work hard helped her overcome personal challenges, including becoming a mother while in college and a divorcee in her twenties. Lori's ability to reflect on her own shortcomings as a manager helped her become a better leader. Today, she is most proud of how she triumphed over adversity to become a role model for others.

GERRI MASON HALL,
Chief Diversity and Social Responsibility Officer, Sodexo

If you work for a truly diverse company, thank people like Gerri. She has made a profound impact on diversity efforts in the corporate world. Her tenacious and unflappable nature helped her overcome feelings of isolation and the inquiries from incredulous white classmates and colleagues about whether she earned her achievements. In her careers in government and private industry, Gerri had to continually prove herself as one of the few women of color at the table. Her goal is to change that particularly demeaning feeling of isolation for future generations.

HAZEL-ANN MAYERS,
Former Executive Vice President and Chief Business Ethics and Compliance Officer, CBS

Hazel-Ann, born in Brooklyn to Barbadian immigrants, has followed her gut instinct even when it made her risk disapproval from others. She switched from studying architecture to pre-law despite her father's objections and eventually made it to Harvard Law School. After getting her degree there in 1999, she worked at two law firms for four years. Eventually, she felt her career aspirations lay elsewhere, and she joined entertainment broadcaster Viacom Inc.'s legal department in 2003. She defied expectations for women of color in business when she stopped relaxing her hair long before natural hair became fashionable. For nearly twenty years, Hazel-Ann has held various roles with CBS and its book publishing subsidiary, Simon & Schuster. Her grasp of her authentic self has allowed her to persevere through adversity.

RAJA AL MAZROUEI,
Executive Vice President of FinTech Hive, Dubai International Financial Centre

Raja was born in 1976 in the United Arab Emirates to a very conservative family, who expected her to pursue the traditional path of early marriage and children, and little contact with men outside the family. Inspired by the career women she saw on TV, and driven by challenge, Raja became the only woman in the family to pursue a career. She overcame cultural expectations for women—including the arranged marriage her family had wanted for her—and launched a technology career, which required working with men. She was accepted into Harvard's Advanced Management Program, which took her to the United States. "I never let go of that vision that I would be a career woman and create something to make an impact and contribute to the development of my community," she says.

SYLVIA METAYER,
Chief Growth Officer,
Sodexo

Sylvia's family was wealthy, internationally traveled, and highly educated, with big expectations for their daughter. She had her own internal drive as well, which led her to follow her inner compass and pivot when necessary—from medicine, to education, to an MBA. When her accounting-firm employer accused her of a "lack of gravitas" after her second child was born, Sylvia switched to a career at the food giant Danone, and then at Mattel, Vivendi Universal, Houghton-Mifflin, and Sodexo. Sylvia attributes the success she's achieved over her long career to being extremely open not only to change but also to differences between herself and others. She values risk over certainty and believes even her failures have been crucial to her success.

BONGIWE NTULI,
Chief Financial Officer and Executive Director, The Foschini Group

Bongiwe was born in South Africa during apartheid, and her mother, a nurse, had to hide the pregnancy or risk losing her job. Bongiwe understood adversity from a very young age. However, she excelled in school, and it served her well when apartheid ended and she received a scholarship from one of the world's mining giants, Anglo American PLC. She became one of the first twenty Black chartered accountants in South Africa and steadily rose through the ranks at Anglo American and other mining companies, then a shipping company, and then The Foschini Group (TFG), a leading African fashion retailer. Her philanthropic work with South African schools has given her a way to help others. "I believe that education is power, and I have been fortunate to have a good education and a belief that I can do anything," she says.

ANDI OWEN,
President and CEO, Herman Miller

Andi's worldview was shaped when she lost her father to leukemia when she was just seven years old. "When you experience something like that as a kid, you don't fully understand all of it. But it does change how you think about life, how you think about the permanence of things, and what you take for granted and what you don't take for granted," she says. This insight into life has served Andi well as she built a career at Bloomingdale's, at Gap Inc., and now at Herman Miller, the $2.6 billion furniture manufacturer. Along the way, she has handled many personal challenges, including a divorce. Now in a season of life when she understands the inherent tradeoffs of being a mom and an executive, she doesn't demand perfection of herself in either realm.

RACHANA PANDA,
Vice President and Country Group Head for Communications, Public Affairs, and Sustainability for South Asia, Bayer

Rachana grew up in India surrounded by strong women and a father who encouraged her to transcend the cultural expectations of her country. By the time she graduated from college, she was confident in her ability to speak up for herself and handle difficult situations. She would encounter many of them as she ascended to the C-suite: moving to the teeming metropolis of Delhi; changing careers from zoology to management; dealing with the early death of her father; having to leave her first job; and responding to difficult situations at work. Almost two decades later, she went on to become General Electric's Chief Communications Officer for South Asia, where she emerged a strong leader. After an eventful stint at GE, she moved to Bayer in September 2020. Rachana's resilience, flexibility, and capacity for introspection make her a role model for other women.

AZITA SHARIATI,
Group CEO, AniCura

Azita's parents encouraged her from a very early age to think for herself, even allowing her as a toddler to pick out her own shoes. As the oldest grandchild in a very large Iranian family, Azita always gravitated toward leadership, organizing performances starring her cousins to delight their elders on family vacations. Her independence and confidence built a resilience that helped her weather the Iranian Revolution, when she was forced to move from a liberal, coed school to a strict Islamic all-girls school. Later, she found the resolve to move to Sweden, learn a new language and culture, and ascend the ladder at Sodexo with encouragement from a woman executive there. As the CEO of Sodexo Sweden, she made sure 50 percent of senior positions in the company were held by women.

MA. VICTORIA (MARIVIC) SUGAPONG, Chief Operating Officer at IE Medica, Inc. / MedEthix, Inc.

Victoria grew up in a modest, Roman Catholic household in Manila, Philippines, as a self-described "conscientious person," which gave her "a purpose in life to a certain extent." Her academic and professional life were successful because she made very thoughtful choices: pushing herself to succeed in school to honor her parents; working her way up the ladder at Manila Water Company and Healthway Medical Clinics; and shifting to a different sector and function at IE Medica and MedEthix. She always chose to be as focused and present for her family on evenings and weekends as she was at work, where she was surrounded by male colleagues who seemed to work all the time. "Success is not measured by the amount of wealth accumulated or the position in the company," she says. "Success is being able to make a difference in this world by making the lives of others better."

DEBBIE WHITE,
Former CEO, Interserve Group Limited

Asked by the UK government in 2020 for help in establishing a network of COVID-19 testing centers, Debbie has been breaking the glass ceiling her entire life. Her experience shows the influence of a supportive family, both in childhood and in adult life. Debbie's working-class parents believed in hard work and in education, and her husband and children readily relocated to support her early career moves. From 2017 to 2019, she was CEO of Interserve Group Limited, a $3 billion UK-based company that provides support, construction, and equipment services to organizations worldwide. After executive jobs at Arthur Andersen, AstraZeneca, Sodexo, and Interserve, Debbie has had the chance to follow her passion for improving women's health. She is a trustee of Wellbeing of Women and was recently appointed their treasurer.

ZHEN WU,
Vice President of Legal Services, Asia,
Magna International Inc.

Zhen's career began in 1995 at a Shanghai investment consulting firm, and since then she has risen to legal positions at multibillion-dollar confectionary maker Perfetti van Melle, the international law firm Bird & Bird, General Electric, and now Magna, a $39 billion international automotive supplier. Though she has weathered some tough years—from the struggles that come with a long-distance marriage to being a working, single mother—Zhen is at peace with the way her path has unfolded.

Chapter 1

CAREER

"Respect all jobs but find one that gives you joy and purpose; make sure your contribution is valued."

—ETABA

In November 2018, celebrated actress Viola Davis, who won the Best Supporting Actress Oscar for *Fences* a year earlier (and who has also earned an Emmy and two Tony awards), sat down with journalist Tina Brown to discuss her role as a Black woman in the entertainment industry.[12] Davis pointed out that despite the accolades that have led many to call her "the Black Meryl Streep," she still has to play hardball with producers to make sure she is paid what she's worth—and her salary is far less than that of celebrated white actresses in her echelon, like Streep, Julianne Moore, and Sigourney Weaver.

---

12 "WITW L.A. Salon: Viola Davis on being told she's 'a black Meryl Streep,'" Women in the World, February 14, 2018, https://www.youtube.com/watch?v=Sf0kDGVkVzQ.

Davis's experiences, like those of the successful business-women whom you'll encounter throughout this book, show us how time and again the accomplishments of women—especially women of color—are undervalued and unrecognized. Given the caliber of women I convened, as you look at their lives and mine, you may think that "career" is the one thing that every one of us has mastered. But there is much more to this dimension than obtaining a certain job title, pay grade, or type of office. One of the greatest commonalities I found with my peers is that our idea of a successful career can, and does, change drastically depending on what stage of our lives we are in. There is no single destination, nor is there a single pathway. For a dimension that seems so straightforward, it may actually be the most personal and nebulous of all.

Women, especially women of color, face numerous challenges in attaining a top post at a large organization. In many cases, these challenges force women into unintended choices, made out of expedience or the feeling that they have no other options. The section below outlines these problems. Then, we will present stories of businesswomen's journeys and the *deliberate* choices they made that led to professional and personal growth. Finally, I'll offer key takeaways that you can consider implementing in your own life.

CHALLENGES

Women confront many problems and challenges in building their careers, but these five are the most common:

Lower pay and lack of access to good positions

Data continually reveals that while women make up more than half the labor force in the United States and earn more than half of the advanced degrees, we "bring home less pay and fill fewer seats in the C-suite than men, particularly in male-dominated professions like finance and technology."[13] Sadly, statistics reveal that capable women are frequently lower down in the managerial ranks and the pay grades than comparable men.

Well, what if we just "lean in" as Sheryl Sandberg recommends in her blockbuster book of the same name? Here, data is catching up to what a lot of women have already known: the "girlboss" craze sold a lot of branded coffee mugs and laptop cases, but left women with brand new performance pressures in a world of work that is still rigged in favor of men. Even if the "lean in" and "girlboss" mentalities worked, their best-case scenario still perpetuates a dangerous worldview. As Amanda Mull put it in her *The Atlantic* elegy, "The Girlboss Has Left the Building," "When a country is grappling with mass death, racist state violence, and the unemployment and potential homelessness of millions of people, it becomes inescapably clear that when women center their worldview around their

---

13 The latter is according to a study published in February 2019 in Harvard Business School's Working Knowledge.

own office hustle, it just re-creates the power structures built by men, but with women conveniently on top."[14]

Women have long been told that if we stand up, be remarkable, outperform everyone, dress impeccably, and speak in warm, honeyed tones, we will "make it." But nothing has shattered "the glass ceiling," the girlboss concept's precursor. According to McKinsey's "Women in the Workplace" report, entry-level women are 18 percent less likely to be promoted than their male peers; if entry-level women were promoted at the same rate as entry-level men, the number of women at the senior vice president and C-suite levels would more than double.[15] Men are often not even aware of the gender skew; they think representation is just fine at their companies. In companies where only one in ten senior leaders is a woman, nearly 50 percent of men felt women were "well represented" in leadership, according to *Harvard Business Review*.[16]

Women of childbearing age deal with the added complexity of organizing and managing childcare. We must touch on that as well, for that is when most women drop off the career ladder or settle for less to accommodate new responsibilities.

---

14 Amanda Mull, "The Girlboss Has Left the Building," *The Atlantic*, June 25, 2020, https://www.theatlantic.com/health/archive/2020/06/girlbosses-what-comes-next/613519.

15 Sarah Coury, Jess Huang, Ankur Kumar, Sara Prince, Alexis Krivkovich, and Lareina Yee, "Women in the Workplace 2020," McKinsey & Company, September 30, 2020, https://www.mckinsey.com/featured-insights/diversity-and-inclusion/women-in-the-workplace.

16 Anne Welsh McNulty, "Don't Underestimate the Power of Women Supporting Each Other at Work," *Harvard Business Review*, September 3, 2018, https://hbr.org/2018/09/dont-underestimate-the-power-of-women-supporting-each-other-at-work.

Discrimination

Women of color have it worse than white women. The racial prejudice Black women have experienced is impossible to ignore. According to Coqual's report, "Being Black in Corporate America: An Intersectional Exploration," "Black professionals are more likely than white professionals to be ambitious, yet nearly one in five feels someone of their race/ethnicity would never achieve a top job at their companies."[17] The study also found that over 61 percent of Black professionals working in the continental United States have experienced racial prejudice at work, and less than half of all professionals think their companies have effective diversity and inclusion efforts.

In an oral history of Black Wall Street professionals compiled by *Bloomberg Markets,* former Lehman Brothers employee Brigette Lumkins spoke of feeling painfully uncomfortable at work. "I was perceived as a diversity hire and I think that was part of the resentment against me," said Lumkins, who worked for the firm from 2006 until it closed after the 2008 financial crisis. "I had a lot of stress related to being pigeonholed or being stereotyped as 'combative'—that was the word."[18]

Women of color are largely kept out of the top ranks of organizations. McKinsey's 2019 "Women in the Workplace" report found

---

17   "Being Black in Corporate America: An Intersectional Exploration," Coqual, 2019, https://coqual.org/reports/being-black-in-corporate-america-an-intersectional-exploration.

18   Kelsey Butler, "A Banker Says Being Seen as a Diversity Hire Caused Resentment," *Bloomberg Markets,* August 3, 2020, https://www.bloomberg.com/news/articles/2020-08-03/a-wall-street-banker-says-being-seen-as-a-diversity-hire-caused-resentment?sref=pHsFVc06.

that representation of women in the C-suite went up 24 percent from 2015 to 2019—but representation for women of color at the top was stagnant.[19]

The barriers start early in the careers of women of color, and those in entry-level jobs suffer most when a crisis hits, such as the coronavirus pandemic. Research conducted in April 2020 by the Fawcett Society, a UK-based advocacy group for gender equity, found that four in ten women of color said they would struggle with debt over the next three months.[20] Women of color worried more about going out to work during the pandemic, and 45 percent said they couldn't manage the different demands on their time. Their life satisfaction and happiness were ranked lower than those of other groups.

Lack of allies in the C-suite

The good old boys' club is not helpful. In 2019, research from Northwestern University and Notre Dame demonstrated that women can have similar qualifications and work experience to men, but without an inner circle of close female contacts, it's near impossible to "achieve the executive positions with the

---

19   Jess Huang, Alexis Krivkovich, Irina Starikova, Lareina Yee, and Delia Zanoschi, "Women in the Workplace 2019," McKinsey & Company, October 2019, https:// www.mckinsey.com/-/media/McKinsey/Featured%20Insights/Gender%20 Equality/Women%20in%20the%20Workplace%202019/Women-in-the-work-place-2019.pdf.

20   "Coronavirus: Impact on BAME Women," Fawcett Society, Spring 2020, https:// www.fawcettsociety.org.uk/coronavirus-impact-on-bame-women.

highest levels of authority and pay."[21] Men have the old boys' clubs to hook them up with connections. According to economist Sylvia Ann Hewlett, men are "46 percent more likely to have a higher-ranking advocate in the office [than women]," which "makes an increasing difference in representation as you go up the org chart."[22]

Family and home constraints, especially for women of color

Career women who are also partners and/or mothers often have to manage different kinds of career pressures from within their organizations, as well as within their nuclear families and, sometimes, within their own heads. According to a Pew Research Center Social & Demographic Trend survey, 51 percent of working women with children under age eighteen report that being a parent has made it harder to advance in their career, compared to just 16 percent of men in the same situation.[23]

21 Yang Yang, Nitesh V. Chawla, and Brian Uzzi, "A network's gender composition and communication pattern predict women's leadership success," PNAS, February 5, 2019, https://doi.org/10.1073/pnas.1721438116.

22 Anne Welsh McNulty, "Don't Underestimate the Power of Women Supporting Each Other at Work," Harvard Business Review, September 03, 2018, https://hbr.org/2018/09/dont-underestimate-the-power-of-women-supporting-each-other-at-work#:~:text=Don't%20Underestimate%20the%20Power%20of%20Women%20Supporting%20Each%20Other%20at%20Work,-Anne%20Welsh%20McNulty&text=By%20contrast%2C%20men%20are%2046,go%20up%20the%20org%20chart.

23 "On Pay Gap, Millennial Women Near Parity—For Now," Pew Research Center's Social & Demographic Trends Project, December 11, 2013, https://www.pewsocialtrends.org/2013/12/11/on-pay-gap-millennial-women-near-parity-for-now/#the-balancing-act.

Moreover, a 2018 report by the National Partnership for Women & Families, which drew on research from dozens of scholarly studies, points out that women of color—including 81 percent of Black mothers, 67 percent of Native American mothers, and 52 percent of Latina mothers—are the primary or sole breadwinners for their families, compared with 50 percent of white mothers. Other findings from that report: only 25 percent of Latinas and 43 percent of Black mothers reported having access to paid or partially paid parental leave, and women of color suffered more chronic health problems linked to chronic stress due to everyday racial and gender discrimination.[24]

Another Pew Research Center study, from 2018, noted that more than a quarter of Black, Hispanic, and Asian US residents lived in multigenerational households in 2016, increasing the odds that female breadwinners of color would be caring for both younger and older generations.[25] And a LeanIn poll showed that the coronavirus pandemic made the imbalance even worse for women of color, with 75 percent of Black women and Latinas saying they were spending twenty-one or more hours a week on housework, compared to 55 percent of white women.[26]

---

24 "Paid Family and Medical Leave: A Racial Justice Issue–and Opportunity," National Partnership for Women & Families, August 2018, https://www.nationalpartnership.org/our-work/resources/economic-justice/paid-leave/paid-family-and-medical-leave-racial-justice-issue-and-opportunity.pdf.

25 D'vera Cohn and Jeffrey S. Passel, "A record 64 million Americans live in multigenerational households," Pew Research Center, April 5, 2018, https://www.pewresearch.org/fact-tank/2018/04/05/a-record-64-million-americans-live-in-multigenerational-households.

26 "Women are maxing out and burning out during COVID-19," LeanIn.org and Survey Monkey, May 7, 2020, https://leanin.org/article/womens-workload-and-burnout.

Self-defeating attitudes and behaviors

Women hold themselves back and hesitate to plunge in. Many lack clear career goals and don't work in environments that facilitate their success or their ability to be intentional. An oft-quoted Hewlett-Packard internal report statistic says that women tend to only apply for jobs they are 100 percent qualified for, while men tend to apply for jobs they are 60 percent qualified for.

Some of the women I spoke with suggested that the internalized feelings of inferiority, often specific to our gender, hold us back in ways men generally don't even consider when weighing whether to go for a career opportunity. Sometimes this comes down to an imbalance between soft skills—the people skills generally attributed to being a productive employee and a good team player—and hard skills, which are teachable and measurable. While women in top positions absolutely must have both, work culture can skew the ways they use them.

In my conversations with the women featured in this book, most of them talked freely about the many challenges they faced in being among the first—if not *the* first—women to hold certain roles within their companies. Most of us experienced adversity for being different. This went with the territory: we are all women of a certain age, from all over the globe, and across corporate sectors, so we have often occupied positions and spaces no one like us had ever occupied before. We all dealt with these challenges in different ways, and I believe our perspectives will inspire you as you face your own challenges.

Whatever measure of success I have achieved in my career, it would not have been possible without the incessant struggles for justice and equality African Americans of past and present have waged in the United States. They helped achieve major milestones such as the Supreme Court's *Brown v. Board of Education* decision in 1954, the Civil Rights Act in 1964, and the Voting Rights Act in 1965. Such acts have weakened a legally sanctioned segregation that bound Black people to second-class citizenship.

But as the turmoil of 2021 has shown, plenty of inequality remains. The struggle continues to make America a place where we are all respected and racial integration is viewed with pluralist acceptance.

Whether or not I acknowledged them at the time, I have experienced many unpleasant events. Despite working very hard throughout my career, I have had people in organizations openly question my promotions and tell me they were based not on merit but on the company's desire to check the diversity box. Those remarks were hard to ignore.

The women I spoke with told me similar stories. Tracey Gray-Walker, CEO of American Veterinary Medical Association (AVMA) Trusts, told me, "I'll never forget when one of my CEOs said to me, 'How do I find more people of color like you?' I said, 'I guess you have to be open and give people a shot. I also think you have to support people and it starts by recruiting more people of color. Some are going to wash out...so do the white men. You hire people, they come in, some stay, and some don't. It's no different.'"

It took Tracey many years before she felt she could be her authentic self in the workplace without being unfairly penalized for it. She says it was not uncommon to hear male executives say something she would say verbatim, spoken in the same tone of voice—but "only from [her] would it be seen as threatening."

Tracey recalls one meeting with a roomful of executives, when a man accused her of yelling at him. "We were in a large room. I have a big voice and I was projecting. He was a six-foot-three white man and was a little put off that my voice rose." Tracey explains that men do it all the time, "but I always felt I needed to determine who I wanted or needed to be before I entered the room every single day. If I'm delivering some good news, I can be excited and verbose. But if I'm delivering bad news, I have to be another way, and if I think they're going to provide feedback or address a topic that require[s] a constructive conversation, I need to be ready to manage or control any and all emotional tone."

In her most recent role as the CEO of AVMA Trusts, Tracey has vowed to be her authentic self. "I walk into every room the exact same way," she says. "In my last board meeting, I had a vendor come in and the vendor had not done what they said they were going to do. I addressed their lack of preparation and a few of my board members came up to me and said, 'Wow, way to go.' I said, 'Just doing my job.'"

Tracey adds, "For them to acknowledge that I did what I did really well, without having to say, 'You were a little aggressive,' or 'Did you have to beat them up?' was a relief. In my prior world that's what someone would have said to me, because I was a Black woman taking on white men. I believe that I have found an environment that is more accepting of who I am and the strengths I bring to the organization."

The biased thinking that implicitly or explicitly characterizes Black professionals as inferior "definitely still exists today," says Hazel-Ann Mayers, former Executive Vice President and Chief Business Ethics and Compliance Officer of the CBS Corporation. Hazel-Ann, the daughter of Barbadian immigrants, grew up in Brooklyn and is a graduate of Harvard Law School. Despite being promoted numerous times within CBS for the quality of her work and holding the General Counsel position at the CBS subsidiary Simon & Schuster, she still regrets one missed opportunity. "After law school, when I started working at law firms, I never considered becoming partner," Hazel-Ann says. "The main reason was that I didn't see people of color in partnership roles—I just didn't think it was possible. I should have trusted my instincts and gone for it and not held back."

That women as talented and accomplished as Hazel-Ann reflexively think they will not be permitted into some professional places signals the extent of the problems we grapple with. Even today, as a top-ranking executive, Hazel-Ann says, "Often when we're about to start a meeting, a person who has not met me before looks at the random men in the room to run the meeting, and the person is then surprised that it's my meeting and I'm running it."

Subha Barry, now CEO of Working Mother Media, shared her sharp insights on being the first woman of color in her wealth management division of Merrill Lynch, where she amassed a portfolio of over $2.5 billion in assets. She was among the top 100 of the 16,000 advisors employed by Merrill Lynch. She recounted stories of talking on the phone with prospective clients who were interested in her ideas. When those same people came to her office to meet for the first time, they would ask to have a different advisor—a man generally, or a person "from the United States" specifically.

"I experienced visceral bigotry and racism in so many ways, and it hurt," Subha says. "And then, I began to look around and I noticed that there was nobody else who looked like me in my office. I went to my manager and I said, 'I've been so successful for you. Why haven't you packed the place with people like me?' And his answer was, 'Subha, I got lucky with you. I'm not pushing my luck again.' And I began to realize, *oh my God, they thought all this success happened with me because I was lucky.*"

Despite the deep-rooted stereotypes that create roadblocks for immigrant women like Subha and other people of color, she prevailed, becoming a top 100 producer at Merrill Lynch as a wealth advisor and then building a multicultural business development unit for them, before becoming their first Global Head of diversity and inclusion. She left them in 2009, became Chief Diversity Officer at the US mortgage market mainstay Freddie Mac, and later landed at Working Mother Media, publisher of *Working Mother* magazine, where she is now President and CEO.

Subha is one of the most resilient women I know. She was the first in her family to move from India to the United States— and she had little encouragement. She has survived cancer six times. She did not let herself be deterred, discouraged, or embittered by the bigotry she experienced at Merrill Lynch. Instead, she decided to chisel out an opportunity to create win-wins. She says, "I began to really think through how I could start to show Merrill Lynch the business opportunity in multicultural communities. I thought, 'You shouldn't have to barrel through brick walls to be successful. You should be able to leverage the same kinds of opportunities as young people who have successful networks through their parents or college fraternities.'"

This came after Subha's first bout with cancer. Before then, her focus had been on becoming the best advisor she could be by being successful for her clients and for herself—financially! After that, "career" meant something quite different: she would measure her success by her ability to enact meaningful change. Subha took her proposal to showcase the opportunity for Merrill Lynch in multicultural communities to her CEO. He agreed to give her the chance, on the condition that she give up the entire book of business she had developed over twelve years—and take a pay cut. She agreed. "It was like dying and growing back again," she said.

That's not just a figurative statement. After she committed to this initiative and her strategic goals for the year, Subha's cancer returned even more fiercely than before. She had to take a six-month leave from work to win this battle. While it seemed that her multicultural initiative would fail under the circumstances, Subha's team did not allow that to happen. They were bound by a commitment to a bigger purpose and mission; she had recruited and nurtured them carefully. And they had bought into her vision.

Subha relishes the memory of that year's annual review. "When I went in, my boss at that time fully expected me to say, 'I've been out for six months. We didn't make our goal, but here's what we did.' And guess what? My team was so amazing that they exceeded the goal that year. The lesson I learned there is that if you surround yourself with great people, they will deliver for you when you may not be able to deliver on your own. Actually, you achieve very little just by yourself. I'm proud of how that team came together and how hard they must have worked, because there was a period of about three months when I literally wasn't even on the phone. I couldn't even talk...I was so depleted after my stem-cell transplant."

Even though her challenges have been greater than many of us will ever have to endure, Subha does not see herself as disadvantaged. In fact, it's her personal philosophy that her life circumstances—being born female in a male-dominated society in India—prepared her for the bias she would find in the American corporate world. "As a woman of color, you can never splice away my experience of growing up in a male-dominated society," she says. "I think that was part of what I really was able to bring to my financial services career. It's so male-dominated that it was like being back among all my male cousins in India again. I just needed to find that cohort of men who, like my cousins and brothers, could get invested in my success and care about me. So, I think I was prepared by how I was raised, where I grew up, and how I learned to interact with men."

Rachana Panda, who today is the Vice President and Country Group Head for Communications, Public Affairs, and Sustainability for South Asia at Bayer, shares a similar experience of aligning herself with men who cared about her well-being. Her career was just taking flight in India when her mother suffered a debilitating stroke. "I called my then CEO to let him know that I was on my way to be with my mother and that I didn't know when I would return," recalls Rachana, who was then working for an Indian organization. "He was very supportive. When I reached my mother after a twenty-four-hour train ride, I learned that he had sent someone ahead to the hospital to be with me. His gesture meant more to me than anything; the support and flexibility were what I needed at that time. He was one of my male mentors throughout my career, and having male allies is very important. I also realized you always have to choose between urgent and important in life. It's all about making the choices confidently."

As Rachana's experience shows, women need male allies, especially in a work culture that discriminates against women. Most women have felt that unconscious bias all too often. In my experience, if a meeting is going on among equals and there's not a secretary present, a woman somehow ends up taking the notes. I am always amazed by this. The men in the room will say, "Oh, she's so much better at it," or "She can type faster," or "She has the best handwriting." And before you know it, she's taking the notes, organizing them, and then distributing them. She may think it's a way to show her value, and it often will earn her the acceptance of the men in the group. But she and her male colleagues may never realize how these situations undermine the power dynamic for women. Chapter 9 of this book explores how supervisors can be better allies to women.

While women in top positions absolutely must have both hard and soft skills, work culture can skew the ways they use them.

Azalina Adham, former COO of Bursa Malaysia, Malaysia's stock exchange, says, "I have the soft skills. One thing I don't have is the instinct to grab what I want. A male counterpart would not think twice before jumping in and grabbing an opportunity. It's not that women are unable to make decisions; I think it's because we're more contemplative."

Azalina says she's observed that women assess whether they can commit the time and resources necessary to complete a job and do it well, whereas, "a guy would jump right in and then think about any gaps afterward. We think about those gaps up front. C-suite women should be more open to risk and not require perfection of themselves or worry about not having every single thing the job requires. We place very high standards and expectations on ourselves. We expect to be able to do it all."

Azalina believes we have to go easier on ourselves and lighten the loads we put on our minds. Most importantly, Azalina feels that the competencies and experiences we gain over the years, and the values that we acquire and hone as a result, give us the foundation to embrace new challenges. Hence, as women, we should rely on our self-belief and bank on our self-confidence.

Like Azalina, Debbie White learned she didn't need to prove she could do it all. It made her a better leader, as I saw for myself when she was my boss at Sodexo.

"In my younger career I was very much a 'just do it' person and quite controlling," says Debbie, the former CEO of Interserve Group, who has also consulted and served as an executive at several companies. "Through leading consulting projects, I learned that you can't do it all yourself and you are dependent on your team to get things done for you. This is quite different from being in a corporate environment. When I realized I could work twenty-four hours a day and 365 days a year and still not get everything done, I learned the importance of empowering your team and other leaders. To be able to let go, you've got to build the right team...and you've got to be able to trust them."

Andi Owen, President and CEO of Herman Miller, also shared her philosophy on the importance of soft skills, as well as hard skills. "When I think about what I spend my time doing, of course I look at the numbers and talk about the financial piece of the business and am constantly aware of it, but I spend most of my time mobilizing and communicating," she says. "I'm on the floor meeting people, talking to customers about the company, and learning. Those soft skills are critical to mobilizing and motivating your organization."

She also shared some thoughts on the differences—perceived or otherwise—between men and women in the workplace. "I don't want to grossly generalize and say 'all men,'" says Andi, "but in my experience, a lot of men whom I've worked with have been much more cautious about giving constructive feedback to women, dancing around the subject. They seem to be afraid of an emotional outburst or tears. Whereas when they give feedback to a man, they'll say, 'Dude, that was bad, don't do that again.' I've had the opportunity to go back to some of my favorite male bosses and mentors and ask why they might not have been direct about something. And when they really reflected on it, it came down to,

'Well, I guess I really felt like I was going to hurt your feelings,' or 'What if you cry? It's going to make me feel uncomfortable.'"

The way we raise our sons and daughters can help mitigate these gender disparities. We can also model for both boys and girls how men and women can balance family and career. My own mother set a wonderful example of this through the way she raised my brothers. Etaba really wanted her sons to understand the plight of women and be sensitive to them. She always talked about that. She would say, "Loving someone doesn't mean that they have to take care of you; loving someone means you have to take care of them and you have to make sure that their wishes are met." Today, my brothers are very supportive of their wives.

When we were all children, Etaba would take a radio or some mechanical thing apart and put it back together to show my brothers that anybody could do that. By taking on tasks traditionally considered masculine, she taught my brothers not to assume certain tasks were only the domain of men. It was her way of saying, "You can't order people around, and you can't tell your sisters to do this or that." She was very clear that a woman's place should be the workplace, not the kitchen—unless her professional life is there.

Rachana emphasizes the importance of role models of both sexes. She told me, "My mother was a teacher. My grandmother was an entrepreneur involved in microfinancing. Back then, being entrepreneurial was not common for a woman; looking back, I picked up some of these traits from my grandmother. Not everyone one meets is a career role model—quite a few are supporters like my mother-in-law, who is my fallback ecosystem in the upbringing of my daughter. That means a lot."

Rachana talks about her job at an Indian company with a male chairman who she says was extremely respectful and supportive of women. "Within six months I was promoted to head of communications for the entire group. Since I was promoted quickly, I started getting strange comments from male colleagues who worked there. The CEO handled this transition very smoothly, which gave me the confidence to continue without paying heed to the murmurs. Some of the biggest sponsors for a woman professional are men," says Rachana.

We need our own networks and communities to provide the often elusive intel about who is hiring, salary ranges, promotion timelines, and even résumé advice. As *Harvard Business Review* notes, "Women seeking positions of executive leadership often face cultural and political hurdles that men typically do not; [women] benefit from an inner circle of close female contacts that can share private information about things like an organization's attitudes toward female leaders, which helps strengthen women's job search, interviewing, and negotiation strategies. While men had inner circles in their networks too—contacts that they communicated with most—we found that the gender composition of males' inner circles was not related to job placement."[27] It should come as little surprise that, according to *Forbes*, study after study shows women who support other women are the most successful in business.

---

27   Brian Uzzi, "Research: Men and Women Need Different Kinds of Networks to Succeed," *Harvard Business Review*, February 25, 2019, https://hbr.org/2019/02/research-men-and-women-need-different-kinds-of-networks-to-succeed.

But even Rachana was eventually let down by her male allies. She tells me that when she was working at a telecom company, she got pregnant and told her boss she needed to take a few months off. "That's when many problems started. There was a communications crisis at work during my seventh month of pregnancy. My job was never the same after that, and I left shortly after my maternity leave ended," she says. While her colleagues' behavior was regrettable, her decision was not. She says, "Spending time with my daughter and my elders at home are my priorities. I consider those urgent, since I don't want to look back with regret that I did not spend enough time with my family."

Like Rachana, Sylvia Metayer, now Chief Growth Officer at Sodexo, struggled at times in a difficult corporate environment. One of her first jobs was at an accounting firm that was unfriendly to women. "I was especially upset with the way management treated me when I started having children," says Sylvia. "After my first maternity leave, things started to change at work and the leadership was very unsympathetic toward me. Then, when I had a second child, I took a minimal amount of time for maternity leave, yet I was told that I would not be getting the promotion that I deserved. They felt that I was not fashionable enough and did not possess the necessary gravitas."

Some women might have stayed and felt stuck, fearing the company was just echoing the industry standard. But Sylvia decided to look elsewhere. It was the best thing she could have done. "I went out and bought three suits and was hired by another company within forty-eight hours," she says. She quit her job and hasn't looked back since.

Azalina Adham strongly considered not returning to work after her maternity leave because she loved being a new mother. She had the support of her husband, whom she describes as "a very supportive partner—he comes from a family where his mom was independent and self-sufficient. She ran a food shop and was also active in the kids' lives." But Azalina says it was her gynecologist who gently nudged her back into the workforce. "His advice was for me to take as much time at home as I needed to have my baby and then go back to work because babies grow up." The doctor suggested that Azalina may have risked losing herself in her child's identity. After six months, she returned to the office.

When her first child was born, in 1988, Subha Barry was a very successful commodities trader in a frenetic work environment. Subha says that because the company had "no formal maternity leave policy, I took sick leave and I went back to work two and a half weeks after giving birth. Thankfully, my husband took a month off. He would come to my workplace, which was close by. I would pump [breast milk] in the bathroom, give him the bottle to take home to the baby—that's how we managed, believe it or not."

When professional women have families, even the moderate risk-taking that a man might consider normal for career advancement has much higher stakes. For example, Lorna Donatone, former CEO of Geographic Regions for Sodexo, recalls a time when her daughter was young and the company she worked for was going bankrupt, so she accepted a job offer from friends and relocated her family from Arlington, Virginia, to Charlotte, North Carolina. The new role proved not to be the right fit.

"I moved with a three-year-old and a husband," she recalls. "It was a poor decision. After six months of being on the project, I wondered what I was doing. At the same time, my husband was in Washington, DC, looking for a job, and we ended up moving back. I was out of work for three or four months looking for a job." Lorna ultimately decided to scale back her career ambitions for a few years to prioritize her family, after she realized how difficult it was to take big professional risks with a child at home.

Other women found themselves going to extreme lengths in pioneering flexible working arrangements to meet the demands of professionalism and motherhood. Gerri Mason Hall, Chief Diversity and Social Responsibility Officer for Sodexo, was fortunate that when her son was a toddler, her employer had a preschool on site, which was rare at the time. "This was before it became popular for employers to support advancing women and think about work-life balance," Gerri tells me. "My son went to work with me. And if I had to work late, a law school friend who worked with me would go downstairs to get my son and bring him up to the office. That worked out very well. Once my son went to school, his dad dropped him off and picked him up. I had a lot of good support. Later, if I had to travel, I could leave my son with my sisters who had children—he loved to be with them."

Bongiwe Ntuli, CFO and Executive Director of The Foschini Group, was the only contributor to this book who is single and childless. She tells me that being single "helped while I was growing my career. I could jump on a plane for a few weeks at a time with no worries. This set me apart from some other women since I had a great deal of flexibility. I have worked largely in male-dominated industries, and especially as I moved up the hierarchy it has allowed me to compete fairly with my male counterparts. I also have opportunities to socialize with my male colleagues." Bongiwe says that a lot of the decisions are not made in the boardroom but outside of it, so the networking with her male colleagues has been useful to her career.

"I had always worked hard with determination and drive," she says, and as a result, "I have missed a few opportunities to have a family. I had always hoped to find someone just as driven and focused as I was. As I get older, I realize there are many aspects of relationships and that success can be measured in other areas. I have a full life. However, if I had been more realistic, I could have had an even fuller life. Success is not determined by only one aspect. Financial achievement is one piece, but I could have done better in other areas such as family and self-care. It's never too late though."

Flavia Bittencourt, the General Manager of Adidas in Brazil, is a woman who at first hesitated to take career risks, but once she did—and found her footing—she actually felt empowered to have more children and become more active in her family life. It all began when she almost missed an amazing career opportunity because she believed that she wasn't the perfect candidate for a position. She had grown her career through roles in finance and telecommunications. Then a headhunter who knew her well, and who had placed her successfully in other roles, called with a new opportunity.

"The headhunter told me about an opportunity to be the CEO for Sephora in Brazil," says Flavia. "My response was, 'Are you joking? I have no experience in retail and no experience in beauty.' She replied, 'When I took you from the bank to telecom, you had no experience in telecom either, and you have a very successful story to tell. Just come in and be part of the process,'" recalls Flavia. "She said, 'If you like the company and the company likes you, I think there's a match.' The headhunter asked me to go home and write an essay on why Sephora should choose me. This was more about convincing myself that I was the right person for the job. I was hired."

Without that woman-to-woman intervention, Flavia would likely never have ended up in her current role. Sephora gave her experience working within a large multinational company and winning over her superiors. "Sephora's other leaders were not in Brazil and they needed to be taught everything about the complexity of Brazil," says Flavia. "That was scary. It took them one year to feel confident in my advice. After that first year, they felt very confident in me."

Few things are more powerful than when women in the C-suite blaze a trail for other women. Flavia has done this. She married her first husband and had children when she was very young, which put stress on her career. Both her mother and her husband thought she should not even have a career. After her first marriage foundered, Flavia remarried and continued to grow professionally. Eventually, she even had two more children. This time, she felt confident being a mother and a successful businesswoman. She says, "When I traveled, I took our nanny with me to watch over my children. When the other women at work saw I had all that power and still could take time to have a baby, they noticed that I could manage both. It seemed every woman at the company became pregnant at the same time after that." Flavia says it was important to her that she be very supportive of her female colleagues.

TAKEAWAYS

As the stories in this chapter illustrate, women in general and women of color in particular face substantial challenges as they work their way into top jobs, but they have found strategies that work for them. Here are some that may inspire you:

1. Build a great team.

Subha Barry's team delivered for her and helped her meet her goals while she was battling cancer. I have often focused on building a great team with diverse backgrounds and experiences. Having a great team gives you the luxury of thinking about the big picture and what is around the corner, as opposed to the day to day.

I also build teams for complementarity. Every member of the team should feel they can leverage others in the team and learn from one another. A team built deliberately and nurtured effectively can accomplish great things. Building teams takes time and requires intentionality.

2. Collect organizational intelligence.

To advance our careers and our lives, we need good information. Sadly, it is often kept from us, either by accident or design. To overcome this, women must build deep and strong relationships in the workplace. Many of my work friends and colleagues have been my eyes and ears throughout my career, and I have been theirs. They gave me honest feedback and shared assumptions others had about me, while advising about how I should address them. I did the same for them. These relationships were a source of pride, energy, and joy.

My external connections have proven equally important. One organization where I built great relationships is the Executive Leadership Council (ELC). I joined ELC over ten years ago. Its members are Black executives no more than two levels away from CEO in Fortune 500 companies. The ELC's primary focus is to nurture and amplify Black excellence and leadership in business. This organization has been a source of support and inspiration to me. I have developed lifelong relationships here, and it has given me access to resources, advice, and other extraordinary members. My classmates at Harvard Business School's Advanced Management Program (AMP) have also been supportive and inspiring. In fact, most of the women I interviewed for this book are friends and colleagues I met through Sodexo, ELC, and the AMP groups.

3. Find male allies.

I have been very fortunate in having highly supportive male allies. Some were bosses, and others were peers who gave me visibility and amplified my voice. These men stood up for me when I was not in the room. They also gave me direct feedback on how to overcome oppositions and assumptions.

I remember one instance when I was asked to take on a sales leadership role. The company's North America CEO, Richard Macedonia, called me just before his retirement and offered to coach me in developing the sales strategy and territory planning. He understood that sharing his direct-selling experiences with me would be very beneficial to me. The two meetings we spent strategizing were critical to my success, and I am forever grateful.

Both Subha and Rachana also successfully found allies who helped them escape some of the toxicity of the office patriarchy. Look for those who share your values and invest your time in creating authentic relationships with them. That will improve your life—and not just at work.

4. Bond with women who support other women.

If we are ever going to bust open the gender and racial disparities in the C-suite, it will be through our support of one another; the examples we set for and with our friends, colleagues, neighbors, and family members; and the opportunities we create for ourselves and one another. Look out for other women and push them to reach higher, the way Flavia Bittencourt's headhunter convinced her to interview for an amazing though initially intimidating job.

As Madeleine Albright, former US Ambassador to the United Nations and US Secretary of State, once said, "There is a special place in hell for women who don't help each other." I have been fortunate to work with, and for, many women who helped me. And I helped them as well.

5. Search for female role models.

Whether or not we've had female role models in our workplaces, we can always learn from the women who have inspired us in other parts of our lives. Remember how Rachana looked to her mother and her grandmother, although they never got to pursue business careers.

At this point in the book, you know that my role model has been and always will be Etaba. But I am also blessed to have my daughter, Helen, and sisters who inspire me every day. The women in this book are my role models as well. You will likely find that no one woman can inspire you in all parts of your life or for every circumstance; I have different women to whom I look for guidance in different situations. I also look to historical figures, my bosses, direct reports, colleagues, friends, and politicians. If a woman has faced circumstances like mine and has achieved what I want to achieve, I study her and learn from her.

Debbie White is one such inspiring woman. I worked with and for Debbie for many years. I was often awed by her authentic and compassionate leadership. I also admired how she made it okay for women to bring their whole selves to work. In meetings of top executives, she often introduced herself as a mother and wife first. She was clear about her priorities and was not afraid to let others know them.

6. Become a role model for other women.

Show other women it's okay to have a life outside work, like when Flavia took time to raise her family and inspired the women in her office to do the same. This sets the pace for women working for us.

7. Raise the next generation to be better.

We can help reverse the disparity between men and women in both work life and home life by modeling healthy interpersonal dynamics for the children in our care. Etaba's influence taught my brothers and me to support each other. Our interactions with our kids need to be intentional, too. I am not saying there is a perfect formula for raising children. Every parent-child relationship and family dynamic is unique. I don't know of any parent who feels that they have done everything perfectly. I know that we do our best with what we know and the resources available to us. As for me, being a first-generation immigrant brings its own complexities, which Etaba did not have to face. However, she raised ten children and I only have one child to raise. Even with one child, I often ask myself what Etaba would have done in certain situations. I know I am a better parent for having her as a mother, but sometimes, I still feel somewhat inadequate—something I am always working through.

Chapter 2

COMMUNITY

*"There are two kinds of friends: those who will be
there for you because you have been there for them,
and everyone else—and you need them all."*

—ETABA

W<small>E ALL NEED A SENSE OF COMMUNITY: THE SUPPORTIVE</small>
network of important relationships outside of work. Your
community may include people who live with you, your family
of origin, relatives, distant friends, nearby friends, neighbors,
and others who share your professional and personal interests.

In the previous chapter, we explored how being a woman, a partner,
and a parent can have an impact on our careers. Here, we will focus
on how the quality of our interpersonal relationships—the strength
of our "community," as I refer to it—greatly impacts our success
both in and outside of work. The community dimension is particularly important. When our interpersonal relationships are out of
balance, it affects all aspects of our lives. We need to be deliberate in
how we choose, build, and nurture these relationships. We also need
to know when to walk away from relationships that do not work.

61

In general, people who cultivate good relationships are happier and live longer. When the contributors featured in this book were missing a strong sense of community, they also experienced dissatisfaction with other dimensions of their lives, such as self-care and growth. This reminds me of the work of Dr. Edward M. Hallowell, who literally wrote the book on why people must connect with others. In *Connect: 12 Vital Ties that Open Your Heart, Lengthen Your Life, and Deepen Your Soul,* he asserts that human connection is as critical to our health as essential vitamins, yet is increasingly challenging to achieve as society becomes busier and less connected.[28] Connection, he believes, is more than access to the internet; without person-to-person connection, our health suffers. We need connections to people, groups, neighborhoods, clubs, and organizations.

Communities make us better citizens and better people. Robert Putman wrote, in *Bowling Alone: The Collapse and Revival of American Community,* "In the last third of the 20th century, institutions that served as glue for human connections are attracting fewer participants: churches, professional organizations, informal clubs, bowling leagues, community organizations like PTAs."[29] He argues that civic engagement has suffered because of it. He calls these places "the load-bearing beams of our civic infrastructure." Without them, we are stunted.

Loneliness can be just plain deadly. In a stunning and widely read *Harvard Business Review* article in 2017, US surgeon general

28 Dr. Edward M. Hallowell, *Connect: 12 Vital Ties that Open Your Heart, Lengthen Your Life, and Deepen Your Soul* (New York: Gallery Books, 2001).

29 Robert Putnam, *Bowling Alone: The Collapse and Revival of American Community* (New York: Simon & Schuster, 2000).

Vivek Murthy pointed out that 40 percent of US adults feel lonely, including half of CEOs.[30] The actual number is probably higher. Loneliness can have the equivalent life-shortening effect of smoking fifteen cigarettes a day and is even more deadly than obesity, Murthy says. Even women with partners or children can be silently suffering from loneliness if their partners aren't providing support both emotionally and in maintaining the home. This is where other people in a woman's "community" become vital; they can help women enjoy a richer, more satisfying life—even women who don't find the home front a source of strength. A 2017 University of Texas at Austin study found that strong friendships provide a buffer from the stress of marital problems.[31]

Women have a deeply wired need for connection. A 2002 UCLA study revealed that when women experience stress, they instinctively seek to bond more closely with others, including their children and friends.[32] This closeness stimulates the release of the hormone oxytocin, which reduces stress.

One of the biggest barriers to fostering a strong community is a lack of time. It's hard to nurture relationships outside of work, given the demands of executive jobs—and all jobs to be found

---

30 Vivek Murthy, "Work and the Loneliness Epidemic," *Harvard Business Review*, September 26, 2017, https://hbr.org/2017/09/work-and-the-loneliness-epidemic.

31 Elizabeth Keneski, Lisa A. Neff, and Timothy J. Loving, "The Importance of a Few Good Friends: Perceived Network Support Moderates the Association Between Daily Marital Conflict and Diurnal Cortisol," *Social Psychological and Personality Science*, September 14, 2017, https://journals.sagepub.com/doi/10.1177/1948550617731499.

32 Shelley E. Taylor, Laura C. Klein, Brian P. Lewis, Tara L. Gruenewald, Regan A. R. Gurung, and John A. Updegraff, "Biobehavioral responses to stress in females: Tend-and-befriend, not fight-or-flight," *Psychological Review*, July 2000, http://www.anapsid.org/cnd/gender/tendfend.html.

along the path to the top. It's easier, of course, to nurture relationships when work isn't all-consuming. According to Gallup's "Women in America: Work and Life Well Lived" report, women who are out of the workforce have higher social well-being. Criteria for social well-being included whether a relationship with a spouse, partner, or close friend was doing better than ever and whether friends and family gave the respondents positive energy every day. In discussions with the contributors to this book, I saw right away that those who prioritized community and had confidence in the strength of their community did in fact put significant effort into nurturing relationships that brought them joy—with partners, children, neighbors, or even old childhood friends.

Being consumed by taking care of many family members can also prevent women from forging communities of support. When women feel pressure from all sides to take care of everyone, they can't be proactive about building other supportive and nurturing relationships. In the *American Economic Review*, Claudia Goldin reveals that women, more than men, seek full-time jobs compatible with their domestic lives.[33] Many of us care for children, aging parents, even siblings or other family members with special needs. That can mean forgoing career opportunities our male colleagues would seize without a second thought.

Women have stumbled upon many ways to balance and compartmentalize their lives so that they can be fully present both at the office and at home. But skills such as sharing the domestic burden

---

33 Claudia Goldin, "A Grand Gender Convergence: Its Last Chapter," *American Economic Review,* 2014, http://econweb.umd.edu/~davis/eventpapers/GoldinConvergence.pdf.

with a partner are often only learned through experience. I have often found that people take what you give. Unfortunately, if we are taught to be great mothers or spouses, we find ourselves being stuck with everything. For example, if a woman continues to handle all the domestic tasks and keeps her husband disengaged from them, he will often get comfortable with this.

In our household, my husband is the one who takes out the trash and ensures the bins are ready to be picked up on trash removal days. The only time I think about the trash removal process is when my husband is away. I notice, then, the thankless but essential part of his household responsibility. But, similarly, I do many other seemingly small but time-consuming tasks every day without making a big fuss. I am not saying these activities should be debated or assigned daily, but we need to acknowledge each other's efforts, as lack of recognition can cause frustration and derail all types of relationships.

Clearly, more women than men do most of the housework and are the primary caregivers to their children and possibly elderly parents, while also holding full-time jobs. And in too many companies, women get penalized for being caretakers at home. Businesses often don't accommodate busy working mothers, who often feel forced to make a choice. Kathryn Sollmann, author of *Ambition Redefined: Why the Corner Office Doesn't Work for Every Woman & What to Do Instead*, writes that "a woman forfeits up to four times her salary for every year out of the workforce."[34] Even those who have the means to hire someone to come in to assist—babysitters, home healthcare workers,

---

34 Kathryn Sollmann, *Ambition Redefined: Why the Corner Office Doesn't Work for Every Woman & What to Do Instead* (New York: Mobius, 2018).

house cleaners—bear the responsibility of delegating and over-seeing domestic labor. One of the biggest obstacles facing us in C-suites around the world is female- and family-unfriendly poli-cies that can make it difficult to stay at jobs and be considered for promotions.

These challenges are even worse for women of color, who earn 19 percent less money than white women, according to a report by the Economic Policy Institute.[35] This wage gap for women of color holds even among women with college educations.[36] So even when women of color can get paid time off to take care of loved ones, they suffer more because most family-leave plans only provide a portion of their (usually smaller) salaries.

Women of color also struggle with cultural expectations of "doing it all." Kimberly Seals Allers, in a 2018 article in *Slate,* wrote: "Historically, we have always worked and mothered. Many have even grown up seeing their mother and grandmother work more than one job. This is all we know. So the notion of having time to mother feels unfamiliar. There is still the social stigma of taking time off to mother—something black and brown women have never felt free to do."[37]

---

35   Elise Gould and Jessica Schieder, "Black and Hispanic women are paid substan-tially less than white men," Economic Policy Institute, March 7, 2017, https://www.epi.org/publication/black-and-hispanic-women-are-hit-particularly-hard-by-the-gender-wage-gap.

36   Richard V. Reeves and Katherine Guyot, "Black women are earning more college degrees, but that alone won't close race gap," Brookings, December 4, 2017, https://www.brookings.edu/blog/social-mobility-memos/2017/12/04/black-women-are-earning-more-college-degrees-but-that-alone-wont-close-race-gaps.

37   Kimberly Seals Allers, "Rethinking Work-Life Balance for Women of Color," Slate, March 5, 2018, https://slate.com/human-interest/2018/03/for-women-of-col-

Research has shown that, burdened by all this and more, women of color are more prone to emotional and health problems. "African-American Women and Work-Life Balance," a 2018 study by Alisha Diane Powell at Walden University, found that discrimination, racism, and classism make work-life balance harder to achieve for women of color.[38] This makes them prone to depression, anxiety, and other health problems. In addition, she cites research that shows African-American women have higher incidences of divorce and marital instability, which puts more financial pressure and stress on them. Women of color have fewer resources than their white counterparts to deal with this at the office. Melinda Gates, Co-chair of the Bill & Melinda Gates Foundation, wrote in a 2017 LinkedIn post, "We're still sending our daughters into a workplace designed for our dads," while "minorities have less access to networks, mentorship, and resources to help them manage mounting responsibilities at work and at home."[39] Organizations suffer as a result, she added. She called for expansion of pro-family policies like paid family and medical leave.

Since even those of us with the best pay and benefits are only getting 168 hours a week to optimize our lives, I feel it is important to share the stories of women who are both highly satisfied with their lives outside of work *and* looking to make improvements. The upshot: integrating work and community is an

or-work-life-balance-is-a-different-kind-of-problem.html.

38 Alisha Diane Powell, "African-American Women and Work-Life Balance," Walden University, 2018, https://scholarworks.waldenu.edu/dissertations/4941.

39 Melinda Gates, "We're sending our daughters into a workplace designed for our dads," Bill & Melinda Gates Foundation, September 27, 2017, https://www.linkedin.com/pulse/were-sending-our-daughters-workplace-designed-dads-melinda-gates.

ongoing journey that is different for everyone, and even the women who seem the most accomplished don't always have it all figured out.

My own story shows how building a community of supporters can help one through challenges at work and at home. I graduated from high school in Ethiopia in 1981, and a year later I took one of the biggest leaps of my life: I boarded a plane with my brother, Naod, and moved halfway across the world to go to college in Boston, Massachusetts, where my sister DeeDee had been sent in 1973, just before the Ethiopian Revolution. We left our home, parents, siblings, and so many lifelong friends, in pursuit of education and opportunities, not knowing if or when we'd see our loved ones again.

When we arrived, the culture shock was profound: for the first time in my life, I was a foreigner in a new land—a land with different customs, different idioms, different rules, and so many different faces. I had to learn the ropes quickly. I'd grown up surrounded by family and neighbors, never knowing what it was like to be the "only"—the only immigrant, sometimes even the only Black person, in a classroom or a workplace. At just nineteen, I had to create a new community of friends and family for myself.

But I was lucky to have the support of DeeDee, who introduced Naod and me to our new world and showed us how to navigate it. My first instinct when coming to the United States was to seek out fellow Ethiopian émigrés and other people who looked and sounded like me. But DeeDee impressed upon me the need to be open to all people. She told me, "You can always find those who make you feel comfortable to be who you are. But if you want to grow, you need to seek out those who stretch you and make you feel uncomfortable." DeeDee suggested that I integrate myself into the mainstream by seeking out people I wanted to emulate. "Study them," she said. "Spend time where they are spending time. Learn the people, the culture, the lifestyles."

Her advice was not easy to implement, since it was very different from the conversations I was having with my friends at the time. I was often tempted to spend time with these people, doing whatever they were doing. I was not forthcoming with them about my private ambitions, since I was fearful of my friends' judgment of what, at the time, could seem a very unrealistic dream and far from my current reality. As a result, I could not be my most authentic self around these friends, but I struggled at first to seek new horizons. Nevertheless, I respected my sister and knew the importance of her advice. I am sure she was unsure at times whether I would overcome the temptations around me.

Still, DeeDee encouraged me to imagine the biggest, boldest dream possible, and then make it my goal to realize it—even if it exceeded my capabilities at that moment. "Prepare for what you want to become," DeeDee advised. I took her advice to heart.

Growing up in Addis Ababa, I'd always had an easy time making friends in the neighborhood and at school, and I'd enjoyed deep bonds with my cousins. To this day, I value those early friendships because they taught me how to network effectively and build relationships. With the support and counsel of DeeDee, I learned how to be self-sufficient and find my way in any environment, whether or not I felt included.

One of the first things I did was enroll at Mount Ida College in Newton, Massachusetts, to earn my associate degree in biochemistry. I quickly realized that even though I was good at science, it wasn't for me, and I decided to take time off from school. I didn't know what to do, and I was feeling a bit unmoored. Thankfully, my family and my growing community of new friends helped me navigate the way. Following my sister's advice, I took a job waiting tables and bartending in lively Harvard Square establishments in Cambridge, where students and professors from Harvard University and MIT would hang out to study and talk. I worked first at Algiers Café, and later at 33 Dunster Street, a family-style American restaurant where I would eventually find the path that led to where I am today.

A university town like Cambridge—a cultural and intellectual epicenter—brings together brilliant minds from all over the world, and those were the people I wanted to emulate. It was very stimulating to observe my customers as they discussed ideas, culture, current events, and their lives. Waiting on them afforded me an opportunity to interact and engage with them. When I wasn't at work, I'd watch movies and read biographies my customers were talking about, as I sought to understand how they got to where they were. I even listened to the audiobook *The Psychology of Winning* by Dr. Denis Waitley, to learn how to have a purpose, save money, be efficient with my time, and surround myself with people who inspire me.

Some of my most inspiring customers were professors who taught evening classes at Harvard, so I signed up for those classes, not only to enlighten myself and test my limits, but also to access a place that seemed so inaccessible. It might seem strange that waiting tables at a big family restaurant in the heart of a college town is what would lead me to where I am today, but I discovered my passion for business there, and seized every opportunity to take things to the next level. I learned how to be a bartender. And when I was asked to supervise, I spent all night learning the computer system and volunteered to do the financial reports. When the restaurant's general manager left suddenly, I was offered his position because I was the only one who knew how to do his job. I was in my twenties, managing people older than me, some of them twice my age. I didn't have an MBA. I didn't even have an undergraduate degree. It might have intimidated some people, but it invigorated me, at least for a while, because I knew I wanted to push myself further.

When I was asked to run more restaurants, I did so without hesitation. Then I stretched my ambitions even further.

I eventually met my future husband, Shif, a math professor at Temple University. This offered me the opportunity to move to Philadelphia. I went back to school to get my bachelor's degree in organizational management from Eastern University, which I did while working a full-time job. I'd eventually find my way to Sodexo, the company where I evolved for over twenty years, and pursue my education further at Temple University, where I earned an Executive MBA. I later became Sodexo's Global Head of Sales and Business Development and CEO, Healthcare North America, positions I held while raising a daughter, who is now a young adult with her own career. In 2019, I became President of ServiceMaster Brands, a post I held until fall of 2020 (when the company sold).

I got to where I am in large part because I had my community of friends and family to anchor me and show me the way, including a great partner—my husband—who fully supports my pursuits, and my daughter, who inspires my every move. The stories of many of the women I interviewed seemed to wind like the strands of a braid with career, family, and friends creating a beautiful symmetry. This braiding may appear easy, but it takes practice.

Azita Shariati, Group CEO of AniCura, remembers being twenty years old, newly relocated to Sweden, learning a new language, and caring for her newborn son. It was overwhelming at times, but she was fortunate that her husband was an equal partner who encouraged her to pursue her dreams. Years later, with her son grown, Azita realizes that family support is a gift and she prioritizes building relationships with the next generation of her family, including a grandson. "On a personal level, it's important for me to help others be successful," Azita says. "This comes from watching my mom and how she supported those around her. She has always taken care of others."

In reflecting on Azita's comments, I was reminded how lucky I am to have a husband who believed in me and, most of all, believed that raising our daughter was an equal responsibility between us. In fact, he did most of the work. Most days, he took Helen to and from daycare, school, and activities and spent a lot of time with her. Although I am so grateful to have such a partner, I'm often envious of the depth of their relationship. I remember on one of those rare occasions when I went to pick Helen up, her teacher said to another teacher, "Oh, is this the mom?" I wondered if they would say the same thing to the dads who only periodically showed up. There were times when even my girlfriends who have children would say, "Your husband deserves an award." And I would say to them, "How about you? Who gives you an award?"

Hearing these types of comments often made me question my choices to be both a mother and an executive. But very recently my daughter told me that she's so grateful I worked, because I provided her with a great role model and she was exposed to people and places she would not have experienced if it were not for my career. That made me feel better about my choices.

Rachana Panda, Vice President and Country Head for Communications, Public Affairs, and Sustainability for Bayer's South Asia region, also feels a need to be deliberate in her focus on loved ones. She says, "Spending time with my daughter and my elders at home are my priorities. I consider those urgent, since I don't want to look back with regret that I did not spend enough time with my family."

Many of us make decisions about what kind of positions we take on based on the loads we carry at home. This can be seen in the story of Ma. Victoria Sugapong,

Chief Operating Officer at IE Medica, Inc. / MedEthix, Inc. in the Philippines, she is married with two kids. "Being a wife and a mother meant that I had to make certain choices given the demands of these roles, especially during growing-up years of our children," she tells me.

Ma. Victoria traveled frequently when she worked as the CFO of Manila Water Asia Pacific Pte. Ltd. Her commute to and from work was three hours each way in Manila's brutal traffic. As a result, her day was punishingly long. Ma. Victoria says that she and her husband chose to live where they did because they wanted a home setting they could continue to enjoy once they retired. Still, it's a wonder Ma. Victoria was able to summon the energy to cook, engage in conversation, or do anything after such a workday. It was especially difficult knowing she would be doing it all over again the next morning.

"I was fortunate that I had a very supportive husband who had reasonable expectations," she recalls. "But even now, I still have responsibilities at home, which at times make it difficult to cope with a management team composed of mostly men who seem to have no other tasks to attend to after office or during weekends."

Sometimes our decision to pursue full-time careers and raise families takes a toll on our marriages, as it did for Zhen Wu, who once worked as General Counsel at a major electronics company. Her husband had taken a job in the Netherlands and the distance proved to be too much. "I was raising our daughter as a single parent. My husband came back the next year and we decided to get a divorce, which was not very common in Chinese culture," says Zhen.

"I tried as best as I could to bring the family together," she explains. "I didn't want an unhappy spouse with all the other challenges I was facing with raising a daughter and focusing on my career."

Zhen believes things haven't improved much in recent years, either. "This hurdle is universal and persists to this day. Whether you are a full-time housewife or a working woman, it is presumed that you need to take care of your family in addition to what you are doing during the daytime." She says that for many women she knows, fulfilling their family obligations is an integral part of their identities. And this just adds to the pressure.

Sometimes, those closest to us help us the most by letting us go. This was the case for Herman Miller President and CEO Andi Owen. "My ex-husband asked for our divorce. I have since told him it was the greatest gift he could have given me because it opened the door to the next chapter of my life, which I didn't have the courage to open myself," she told me.

Andi later remarried, and gave birth to her son, Owen, when she was forty. Her new partner was far more supportive. And because she had already found success in her career when her son came into her life, she found herself applying a lot of the skills that fostered a happy work life to the project of forging a family and raising her son, who is now fifteen.

"From managing people over the years, you learn what methods work and what methods don't," Andi says. "As a parent, because there's such an emotional attachment to what's going on, you can get to anger or despair really fast. I think we all know that fear and intimidation and anger in a work situation are never successful, right? So when I find myself getting to the point where my emotions are taking over in my home life with my son, it's really very nice for me to click into the other side of my brain and say, 'Let's think about this and ask: what if this were an employee situation, what do you need to find out, and what is motivating him right now? Does he feel heard?'"

It's clear that the business side of Andi's life—managing people—has helped her with the community part, managing her son. "It helps me, as a mom, to separate myself from the sheer frustration of it all," she explains. "It sounds awful to say, but it holds me to a higher level than I would hold myself if I were just dealing with my son without that frame of reference. One of my biggest rules with employees is that you've got to maintain self-esteem whether it's a positive or negative interaction. You want your employee to walk away with their self-esteem intact, and when you look at kids, it's the same thing."

Today, Andi believes her surest measure of success is whether her personal community is thriving. She says, "I am less about material measurements of success and more about family and my friends. Is there happiness and joy and strong family life, and are we all going in the same direction as a family? I feel successful when I've had time to spend with my family, when I've had a chance to sit back and laugh with my friends. I feel successful when we're able to provide; we're comfortable and happy."

For Andi, spending time with her family is incredibly important—she lives in a multigenerational household that includes her husband, her teenage son, and her mother. She says she tries to make sure she's present: "even if my time with my family is limited, being there when we're together is critical."

However, she adds, "This is a hard role and it's all consuming. The demands on your time are different from those of any other job I've had, so I don't have a perfect formula. Sometimes I make decisions that are good for the business and sometimes I make decisions that are not, and the same with my family. I try my best."

The right partner can be a wellspring of support for a successful woman. Lorna Donatone, the former CEO of Geographic Regions for Sodexo, says that her late husband Steve, who was seventeen years older than her and belonged to a generation that held traditional views of women's roles, was extremely supportive of her and her career, and took on a hands-on role at home. This enabled her to accept positions that required a lot of travel. "He would come with me to these external events where 98 percent of board members were men and everyone brought their wives," says Lorna.

"Steve was often the only man [there as a spouse], and he embraced that," she says. "I told him he needed to show up for me to understand it's not just men who are at the top of organizations, it's women too. He embraced all that as opposed to being threatened by my career." Their marriage was a real partnership. Until Lorna's daughter Catherine was sixteen, her father walked her to the bus every day—and she loved it. "Catherine was able to choose her partner wisely since she had such a positive male role model in her life. I was working and dad stayed home, so she did not have the typical viewpoint of women in the workplace. It freed her up to do whatever she wanted," says Lorna.

Steve also helped her keep her values aligned with her actions. "Steve would never let me forget that work was just a portion of life," she says. "It was not the whole thing. It wasn't even the most important thing, and I worked a lot when Catherine was young. I started to travel when she was in high school. But Steve kept me grounded. I explained many times that I didn't have any feeling of something being risky, because he had my back."

Although Lorna's beloved husband has since passed away, she now prioritizes maintaining a community in other ways. She says, "I've got a couple of very active groups of women that I have cultivated and nurtured relationships with. One group is where I live, in Virginia Beach, and the other is a group of women I went to junior high with in Lincoln, Nebraska. There's ten of us, and we reconnected about fifteen years ago and started traveling together. We would do it every three or four years. Then my husband passed away in 2013. I have a home on the river, and I said, 'Why don't you guys come here?' So since then, every year, eight to ten of us get together. It's an incredibly important lifeline of women friends, and staying connected is a priority for me. They're all over the country now, so sometimes I go to their cities and visit them. Both groups of women are really, really important to me, and have helped during tough times." Lorna says she's had some of these friends since she was just fourteen years old.

Gerri Mason Hall, Chief Diversity and Social Responsibility Officer, Sodexo, attributes her success at the Department of Labor to the community of women in her life, a network which she carefully nurtured, and which nurtured her. Born in Washington, DC, with Louisiana roots, Gerri says, "I ended up getting political jobs every two years. A lot of it was the network of these women, supporters who were big in politics. It was also a quid pro quo because I was also very supportive of them, and I understood what was meaningful." She adds, "Anybody who thinks they can do it all by themselves is foolish."

Gerri believes nothing is passive about the relationships she's nurtured within her networks. She stresses that connections in your community must be genuine, not tenuous. "Integrity and family are most important," she says. "As much as I don't enjoy all of my family all the time, proximity to them is important to me. I don't go too long without seeing my sisters or talking to them." And while Gerri says she doesn't need to see her grown son every day, she does need to feel connected to him.

Gerri values authenticity and genuine connections with her friends as well, and as an accomplished woman she is wary of people who are opportunistic. "Many people call themselves my friends but those are not meaningful relationships because there is no integrity," she says. "There are those who reach out to me and I know there's an 'ask' coming. They start with, 'We've got to get together.' And then comes the ask."

Like Gerri, Lori Johnston, Executive Vice President and Chief Human Resources Officer at Amgen, values her network of genuine friends. She restores herself by taking "girl trips." She explains, "I have two girlfriends from Dell. We had been there for each other from the very beginning of our Dell days, and we are still together today. Every year we go somewhere together. For a female executive, having girlfriends is probably one of the best self-care things you can do—women whom you can turn to in life, parenting, being a wife, being a daughter of aging parents, being an executive, being in an all-male environment. You can just be with these girls, and you can support and help one another. These two women are my posse. We are texting or sending things to each other, we're calling each other, we're asking for advice. I think that's probably one of the biggest self-care things that I've done."

Listening to my fellow high-achieving women discuss the great effort of creating authentic community reminded me so much of

Etaba. She seemed to knit deep and rewarding connections with friends and family out of thin air. But only now do I understand how much effort and sacrifice she put into this aspect of her life. When I was growing up, so many times I would come home to find my mother on the couch, surrounded by her women friends. They would be deep in conversation, laughing and interjecting, and I could feel their joyful energy.

In fact, my own friends would come over specifically to see her! My mother made herself available to all her children's friends, helping and advising. She put effort into being fully present to everyone she encountered, remembering what they said about their likes, dislikes, and histories. And in the process, she must have learned everything she needed to know about us—her children—from our friends.

Etaba made her children, their friends, her own friends, and many others feel deeply heard, a skill that would have served her well if she had been able to pursue a career. I didn't realize how true this was until after she had passed away. My mother died in Ethiopia on September 13, 2001. My other siblings in the United States and I could not even hope to go to the funeral, as no planes were flying after the attacks on September 11. Instead, we gathered at my sister's house to mourn and reminisce together.

Etaba not only endeared herself to her children to the point that we revere her, but she also helped us develop very strong bonds with one another that have persisted throughout decades and long separations as a source of strength. To this day, I love talking to my sisters about everything. I talk to my brothers almost every day. My siblings are very supportive, and they are amazing people.

One of my fondest memories is when, as adults, thirteen of us went to the beach. One of my sisters is very meticulous and she brought coffee in a thermos. I thought, "I would never think to bring coffee to the beach!" And she had also brought demitasse cups. She was serving coffee in demitasse cups on the beach, and we were laughing so hard. She was the only person who didn't think it was strange. That's the stuff we do together; my family is my entertainment most of the time.

My own daughter asks, "How come you only had one child when you had all these brothers and sisters?" That's the choice, between career and family, isn't it? Women are held back by so many different factors. We go to work, and we come home and still have our domestic responsibilities. We are expected to work still more. One thing we need to learn is how to let go and allow our families and friends to do for us, knowing that others can do as good a job as we do. We need to make more space for those random moments of joy, like drinking coffee out of demitasse cups on the beach.

TAKEAWAYS

1. Expect strong support from those closest to you.

As women, we need to learn how to let go, delegate, and allow our partners (if we have them) and other loved ones to participate in everything. We have to believe that others can do as good a job as we do. I have been fortunate that my partner, Shif, has always been supportive. And I, in turn, have trained myself to leave my work at work. I have made myself stop responding to work emails the moment I enter my home (unless I am working in my home office) so that I can be fully present with my family. This requires choosing a partner wisely, as Lorna Donatone did. Her late husband supported her and was willing to stay home so she could work. A 2017 *Harvard Business Review* article by Avivah Wittenberg-Cox suggests that highly ambitious women either choose a highly supportive romantic partner or no partner at all.[40]

2. Build strong support outside of your partner.

Even the best partner for you can't meet all your needs all the time. Building a wide circle of meaningful relationships will allow you to have your emotional, intellectual, and recreational needs met more fully and frequently. Also, don't forget that you can't be everything to everyone (or anyone), either! Provide support to your loved ones in the ways that feel most authentic and fulfilling and recognize how valuable your support is when it comes from a genuine place.

3. Develop and nurture relationships that not only affirm you but also push you to be better.

Your partner, friends, and family members may at times tell you things that you don't want to hear, but those will often be the things you need to hear the most. My sister DeeDee pushed me to find friends who weren't like me. As scary as that was to hear, she was right!

---

40 Avivah Wittenberg-Cox, "If You Can't Find a Spouse Who Supports Your Career, Stay Single," *Harvard Business Review*, October 24, 2017, https://hbr.org/2017/10/if-you-cant-find-a-spouse-who-supports-your-career-stay-single.

4. Build space for strong and genuine friendships with other women.

Lori Johnston, Gerri Mason Hall, and my mother have valued their true friends. Beware of people who are friendly with you because they want something. Being helpful to our friends is something we all can aspire to, but if you find yourself always the giver, check yourself. Being on the hook to solve problems for a person who should be able to solve them alone is a recipe for resentment and frustration.

5. Cross-pollinate skills learned at work with skills applied at home, and vice versa.

Remember that Andi Owen used skills she honed in the office while raising her son, including keeping emotionality in check and encouraging her child's burgeoning sense of self as if he were one of her team members at work. Good communication, an ability to set boundaries, and time management will serve you well in most areas of your life. Don't sell yourself short by only intentionally using these skills at work.

6. Stop trying to be perfect with everyone.

Don't expect every interaction to be perfect. We tend to fixate on the things we get wrong, ruminating on what we said or didn't say and replaying our blunders in our heads. This serves no purpose and robs us of our joy. Ninety-nine percent of the time, no one hangs onto our faults as much as we do. Let go or be dragged.

7. Take joy in helping others succeed, and make space for (random) moments of joy.

As women, we have been socialized to give from an empty cup. This is a mental construct that we should all commit to dismantling. We would live far more expansive lives if we focused our efforts on helping those around us have moments of joy and took the time to stop and bask in our own. In a world where women truly support one another, we would be able to share our joy often.

Chapter 3

PLAY

"One has not lived until one learns how to play and laugh until it hurts."

—ETABA

IF I ASKED YOU TO CONSIDER HOW MUCH TIME YOU SPEND playing, I would bet you'd counter with a question of your own: "Aster, who has time to play? I barely have time to get through the day." But we need to play, perhaps more than we realize. And it's not just time spent running around after your kids or grandkids in your home or yard, or those rare long weekends when you get your friends together for barbecues. If you host or attend book club meetings or dinner parties or hang out with friends to play cards, sports, or board games—all of these qualify as play.

But I want to expand the definition of play in ways our adult selves can better appreciate, even respect. Whether play elicits visions of a three-year-old running through sprinklers on the lawn or a fifty-year-old executive enjoying a rare personal day riding a bike around town, the act offers the same release:

In play, we stop forcing outcomes and instead focus on the experience of being present in the moment for the sole purpose of enjoyment.

My personal goal is to achieve a feeling of childlike wonder. Your concept of play may be totally different. Play brings many benefits and strengths, and that's why it's worth scheduling time for it.

BENEFITS OF PLAY

It makes us better leaders.

Three Dutch university researchers of CEOs at top companies discovered that those who blocked out time for leisure activities said it helped them detach from work, manage stress, connect better with employees, and be more resilient—all qualities that improve their performance on the job. In a 2018 *Harvard Business Review* article about the study, the researchers pointed out that Andy Wilson, CEO of the $5 billion-revenue video game maker Electronic Arts, unwinds with Brazilian Jiu-Jitsu; Brian Roberts, CEO of the $100 billion US cable and media giant Comcast, plays competitive squash; and Nick Adkins, CEO of the $15 billion US utility company American Electric Power, plays drums.[41] This is no surprise to people like Dr. Stuart Brown, founder of the National Institute for Play. He says having a

---

41 Emilia Bunea, Svetlana N. Khapova, and Evgenia I. Lysova, "Why CEOs Devote So Much Time to Their Hobbies," October 8, 2018, https://hbr.org/2018/10/why-ceos-devote-so-much-time-to-their-hobbies.

playful side disarms others because humans are biologically programmed to play.[42]

Many CEOs grew up heavily involved in competitive play. According to research by Ernst & Young, 94 percent of women in the C-suite have been athletes at some point in their lives.[43] That makes sense when you consider that teamwork is a foundation of athletics, just as it is for running a business well. It's not surprising that former US Secretary of State Condoleezza Rice plays both golf and piano, or that *Vogue* magazine Editor in Chief Anna Wintour plays tennis before work. Playing sports also can help us hone our ability to accept and concede defeat, strategize, and move forward.

But if you're not competitive, don't worry. Play can mean anything outside of the office that gives pleasure and reprieve from all the pressure. Play can involve painting (former President George W. Bush), baking (former Yahoo CEO Marissa Mayer), playing the ukulele (legendary investor and Berkshire Hathaway CEO Warren Buffett), building with LEGO (soccer superstar David Beckham), or any other absorbing pursuit.

As a kid, I hated to lose. I was not very athletic, so I participated in activities I was good at such as debate clubs and less strenuous sport competitions like hula hoop, jump rope, and high jump

---

42 Stuart Brown, "Play is more than just fun," National Institute of Play and TEDx, 2008, https://www.ted.com/talks/stuart_brown_play_is_more_than_just_fun/details.

43 Kristy Ingram, "Why a female athlete should be your next leader," Ernst & Young, September 23, 2020, https://www.ey.com/en_us/athlete-programs/why-female-athletes-should-be-your-next-leader.

with my siblings and kids in the neighborhood. Looking back, I was careful in choosing the activities that assured me success. Most kids in my age groups, including my brothers, were boys and liked playing soccer, and the teams did not include girls. I never pretended to know much about sports that I did not like or understand. This attitude of mine is still present today. To my husband's and my colleagues' dismay, I don't make a lot of effort to know about soccer, basketball, baseball, football, or golf. Choosing play activities that I enjoy, and not pretending to like what is popular or expected, has served me well in focusing on restoring myself by doing things like having a great conversation with my friends, practicing yoga, or sitting on the beach with a good book.

So, if, like me, you don't enjoy competitive sports, don't worry; just pick something you love that restores you and gives you a sense of release.

It makes us effective.

"We cannot solve our problems with the same level of thinking that created them," said Albert Einstein. Which is to say, we cannot meaningfully resolve issues at work or with family when we are in the thick of them. We need to be able to switch gears for a while, pull ourselves away from the eye of the storm, and approach the problem with fresh eyes. Leisure activities such as hobbies, sports, or unstructured play with family and friends helps us clear our heads and see our lives from another perspective. It's a way to recharge our batteries and hit the reset button.

A study published in 2020 by four business school researchers in France and the United Kingdom found a compelling link between leisure activities and maintaining the mindsets that make for a sustainable career.[44] The researchers found that if people use their strengths and talents while engaging in leisure activities, without taking those activities too seriously, they increase their self-efficacy, defined as "the strength of people's convictions in their own effectiveness." The researchers pointed out that "in an era when careers require individual agility and proactivity to deal with the unexpected, individuals' belief in their ability to perform effectively within their work and career environment is likely to be crucial...to maintain a career in a sustainable way." When we have the courage of our convictions, we can be effective. Play can help us strengthen our convictions.

It gives us confidence.

Dr. Stuart Brown believes play also boosts problem-solving skills. In his widely watched TED Talk, he mentioned organizations like NASA, JPL, and Boeing, which prefer to hire research and development people who have fixed cars or who tinker with objects in other ways.[45]

---

44 Ciara M. Kelly, Karoline Strauss, John Arnold, and Chris Stride, "The relationship between leisure activities and psychological resources that support a sustainable career," *Journal of Vocational Behavior*, March 2020, https://www.sciencedirect.com/science/article/pii/S0001879119301125.

45 Stuart Brown, "Play is more than just fun," National Institute of Play and TEDx, 2008, https://www.ted.com/talks/stuart_brown_play_is_more_than_just_fun/details.

Dr. Brown points to the example of Kevin Carroll, who grew up poor in Philadelphia and has credited a neighborhood playground for helping him transcend his humble roots and become an author, a motivational speaker, and the head athletic trainer for the Philadelphia 76ers basketball team. We are more likely to take risks when the stakes are low. That means our leisure time activities are places where we can experiment and stretch ourselves without worrying about how our colleagues will perceive us. We gain confidence through play because we are likely to repeat the activities we enjoy doing. When we find ourselves learning new songs for the piano or nailing the choreography of our dance classes, we feel better about ourselves and our capabilities.

When we are at work, we—and our colleagues—are far more likely to linger on the one call we mess up rather than the 5,000 tasks we execute successfully. Being in the present while performing activities we love enables us to give ourselves credit for our accomplishments. However, doing activities that keep us humble also helps us keep perspective!

It helps us manage stress.

A 2011 study from the University of Illinois at Urbana-Champaign found that playful, spontaneous individuals reported less stress and better coping skills.[46] In 2007, Australian researchers studied 314 workers and found that those with

---

46   Cale David Magnuson, "The Playful Advantage: How Playfulness Enhances Coping with Stress," University of Illinois at Urbana-Champaign, 2011, https://www.ideals.illinois.edu/bitstream/handle/2142/29611/Magnuson_Cale.pdf?sequence=1.

totally engaging leisure activities recovered fully from on-the-job stress, slept better, and returned to work refreshed.[47]

It helps us in other dimensions.

Play is closely aligned with self-care and purpose, which we will explore in later chapters. When these three dimensions are integrated into our lives, they complement one another and give us the ability to improve our day-to-day and overall outlook, not merely through enlightenment and joy, but also by helping to return us to ourselves. When we feel pulled in many directions, play reminds us of who we are, reconnects us to our core, and brings us a sense of peace.

And when we achieve that sense of peace, we may find that we are ready to take things to the next level, to experience other dimensions.

CHALLENGES TO PLAYING MORE

What holds women back from engaging in play? From my own career and the careers of the women I interviewed, I see five major barriers.

---

47 Peter C. Winwood, Arnold B. Bakker, and Anthony H. Winefield, "An investigation of the role of non-work-time behavior in buffering the effects of work strain," *Journal of Occupational and Environmental Medicine*, August 2007, https://pubmed.ncbi.nlm.nih.gov/17693784.

Time

According to a study by professors at the Vrije Universiteit Amsterdam, CEOs have just 2.1 hours per day for downtime, whether that's relaxing somewhere or pursuing hobbies.[48] Half of the women I spoke with said that play was not one of their top three life priorities.

Too many responsibilities

According to the US Department of Labor, 70 percent of women with children under eighteen are participating in the workforce, and mothers are the primary or sole earners for 40 percent of the households with children under eighteen. Working women with partners also do more household chores than their partners, an average of 60 percent of the unpaid work that goes into running the home. A 2014 study by the Council on Contemporary Families, based on Penn State University research, found that women's cortisol levels, a gauge of stress, actually went up more at home than at the office. Many of the women I've spoken with say that when responsibilities intrude, play is one of the first things to go. It is seen as a frill rather than a necessity.[49]

---

48   Emilia Bunea, Svetlana N. Khapova, and Evgenia I. Lysova, "Why CEOs Devote So Much Time to Their Hobbies," *Harvard Business Review,* October 8, 2018, https://hbr.org/2018/10/why-ceos-devote-so-much-time-to-their-hobbies.

49   "Mothers and Families," U.S. Department of Labor, https://www.dol.gov/agencies/wb/data/mothers-and-families.

We approach play and leisure like a job

The imbalance in responsibilities even extends into vacation times and holiday periods, when everyone should be relaxing but women tend to do more. Mary Bond, author of the *Gutsy Traveler* blog, estimates that women make 80 percent of all travel decisions, even if they are traveling with a husband and family.[50] A 2019 survey of six hundred Long Island residents, taken by Mount Sinai South Nassau Truth in Medicine, found that holiday stress levels are highest for women under fifty, with 61 percent reporting that their stress levels were "high" or "very high" during holidays.[51] They cited family obligations, overscheduling, shopping, and overeating as the causes of their stress.

Screen time

Parents often fret about their children's screen time while not taking their own screen time into account. According to a 2018 Nielsen report, those adults who were surveyed spent nearly half their time each day (on average) interacting with a screen, approximately ten and a half hours.[52] Games and social media

---

50 Geri Stengel, "Reinventing the Travel Experience to Meet the Needs of Women," *Forbes*, March 29, 2017, https://www.forbes.com/sites/geristengel/2017/03/29/reinventing-the-travel-experience-to-meet-the-needs-of-women/?sh=5d383e16fdb6.

51 "Truth About Stress," Mount Sinai South Nassau, November 2019, https://www.southnassau.org/sn/the-truth-about-stress?srcaud=Main.

52 "U.S. Consumers Are Shifting the Time They Spend with Media," Nielson, March 19, 2019, https://www.nielsen.com/us/en/insights/article/2019/us-consumers-are-shifting-the-time-they-spend-with-media.

provide a release of dopamine (the "feel good" hormone), but they can become addictive and time consuming. This cuts into the time for healthier play that clears the head and positively affects sleep, weight, vision, and overall health. Doctors at Scripps Health recommend replacing screen time with physical activity.[53]

Inability to relax

According to a paper published in the journal *BMC Complementary Medicine and Therapies,* between 17 percent and 53 percent of adults have reported "relaxation-induced anxiety," in which they actually feel jittery when they try to relax.[54] Leisure time can help us center and recharge, but many of us feel unable to do it. Project Time Off, an initiative of the US Travel Association, pointed out that Americans accumulated 705 million unused vacation days in 2017 and that only 44 percent of women used all of their vacation time, compared to 48 percent of men.[55] While that may seem only slightly less, consider that women tend to value vacation more: 58 percent of the women said that vacation was "extremely" important to them, compared to 49 percent of the men. And a 2018 survey by the American Psychological

53 "How Much Screen Time is Too Much?" Scripps, February 22, 2019, https://www.scripps.org/news_items/6626-how-much-screen-time-is-too-much.

54 C. Luberto, S. Cotton, and A. McLeish, "OA14.01. Relaxation-induced anxiety: predictors and subjective explanations among young adults," *BMC Complementary and Alternative Medicine,* May 2012, https://www.ncbi.nlm.nih.gov/pmc/articles/PMC3373617/pdf/1472-6882-12-S1-O53.pdf.

55 "Time Off and Vacation Usage (2017)," US Travel Association, 2017, https://www.ustravel.org/toolkit/time-and-vacation-usage.

Association found that one in five people felt stressed out on vacation and 28 percent worked more than they wanted to while vacationing.[56]

Barriers to play are some of the most persistent—screens and the demands of work, home, and family are not going away anytime soon. So, it's up to us to change our mindset and our priorities. I hope the stories that follow encourage you to do just that.

While raising our family and running our farm, my mother, Etaba, seized as many opportunities to tend her garden alone as she did to spend time with friends. She needed both types of play. Etaba also enjoyed playing solitaire while humming her favorite songs to help her relax. She often emerged refreshed and reenergized after a few rounds of the card game. She also encouraged us to build jigsaw puzzles as a family. She would start a puzzle and make it available to whoever was interested. I remember when there were two or three of us working on it at once, taking time off from our studies or whatever else we were doing to unwind by focusing on a fun task together. Now I see my daughter, Helen, doing puzzles and Rubik's Cubes and practicing yoga as alternatives to screen time.

Yet many women say that when things get really busy or stressful, play is one of the first dimensions to get shelved. Among them is Rachana Panda. Rachana says that while she schedules time for yoga and other activities that help her relax, "sometimes those activities get pushed aside." She adds that if she could speak to

---

56 "Vacation Time Recharges US Workers, but Positive Effects Vanish Within Days, New Survey Finds," American Psychological Association, June 27, 2018, https://www.apa.org/news/press/releases/2018/06/vacation-recharges-workers.

her younger self, she would say to take it easy. In particular, she would tell her younger self to make the effort to connect with parents and grandparents before they were gone. And to spend lots of time creating memories with friends and children.

Taking on a more playful attitude can help us take off the blinders that work or our demanding family lives can put on us. When you are playing, you can't take anything too seriously, while, as women in the C-suite, we mostly have to treat our working hours like a matter of survival.

But if we can make the deliberate choice to lighten up, we can see that other dimensions of our lives demand attention, including connecting with the people who have taken a back seat in our lives. So many of our relationships at work are outcome-driven: we need to train those under us to help us achieve our initiatives; we need to cultivate vendor relations to keep a competitive edge; and we need to keep our supervisors informed and watch their backs to maintain good working relations. When we are in the thick of this, we may think about how we ought to call elderly relatives and check in, but this quickly gets pushed aside. But we should absolutely make the effort to call and hear their stories. It's one way to detach from work while building community, though it has a pretty short window of opportunity. We must not mistake what is important for what is vital, and vice versa.

I can hear you asking me, "But what about work?" Rest assured, play and career go hand in hand too. Sandy Lerner, co-founder of computer networking giant Cisco Systems, has chosen jousting as her leisure activity of choice. Meg Whitman, former CEO of eBay, goes fly fishing for fun.[57] Beth Ford, the CEO of Land O'Lakes, studies and advocates for women in agribusiness.[58] Mary Barra, the CEO of General Motors, has said she's too busy to pursue hobbies; however, she keeps toy cars and a bobblehead of Einstein on her desk—perhaps a reminder of the importance of a playful attitude.[59]

I genuinely believe integrating play into work is essential. It is a great way to create an opportunity for team members to get to know one another and build trust. I regularly organize events to play with my team. Before or during strategy or brainstorming sessions, I have taken my teams to museums, hiking, Cirque du Soleil shows, and painting sessions. I've arranged for us to cook together. I have found we perform and think better as a team after such events.

I also integrate playtime into business travel. I make sure that I visit a park, museum, or cultural site, or take a class. Whenever possible, I engage in these kinds of activities with colleagues or friends. I find that this deepens my relationships and expands my networks.

57 Patricia Sellers, "eBay's Secret," *Fortune*, October 18, 2004, https://archive. fortune.com/magazines/fortune/fortune_archive/2004/10/18/8188091/index.htm.

58 Abigail Beshkin, "An Advocate for American Agriculture," Columbia Business School, December 18, 2019, https://www8.gsb.columbia.edu/articles/columbia-business/advocate-american-agriculture.

59 Garrett Parker, "10 Things You Didn't Know about Mary T. Barra," Money Inc, 2017, https://moneyinc.com/10-things-didnt-know-mary-t-barra.

One of my favorite examples of play feeding work comes from Flavia Bittencourt. Prior to her current role, she spent six years in executive leadership at Sephora. Here's a story she shared with me of growing her career there: "When I added Mexico to my portfolio, my boss asked how I would manage my time. I said I would start taking tennis classes to relieve pressure. My kids understand that and are happy that I go to tennis classes and I come home happy. I have to keep my own cup full first."

Zhen Wu, Magna International Inc.'s Vice President of Legal Services, Asia, who lives in Shanghai, explains, "The definition of a successful life is being able to manage all things around me well in [a] multi-dimensional world—so I always reserve sufficient time for hanging out with friends, playing and talking, and pursuing my own interests."

Subha Barry, President of Working Mother Media, has come to a similar conclusion after years of struggling to find time for herself. She says, "When I started in my career journey, I was such a workaholic, but I was also somebody that thought that I had to do it all. There would always be flowers from my garden in the house. I loved to cook. I felt like I had to be the one making all the meals, being the class parent for my daughter and son, planning the family gatherings, etc. So, it got to the point where for a fifteen-year period I was down to sleeping between three and four hours a night."

After multiple health scares over the years, Subha has refined her priorities and her expectations for herself. She embraces the leisurely activities that sustain her through her very demanding work—she loves to cook, to travel, to read. And then, Subha admits, "I have some embarrassing recreational activities. One of my favorite things is to watch home-makeover shows like *Love It or List It*. I love those shows. On weekends, I will watch them and it helps me to relax."

I admit, I can be guilty of the things I warn against. I am naturally inclined to do things for others and for my job, so I don't always remember to prioritize play. It doesn't come naturally to me. However, I've realized that I can achieve everything I want to achieve for my family, for others, and for my job only if I give myself everything I need, including time to play. Tending to our personal needs has a direct effect on our productivity and engagement levels at work and with others. We will delve into this more deeply in the chapters on self-care and growth, but I've come to believe that play helps me achieve my purpose and that it's an important aspect of nurturing the self.

Play, to me, means having the freedom to do anything I want without guilt (though I still do sometimes feel guilty taking time to do things for myself). Defining play as one of my seven dimensions gives me the opportunity to really structure playtime in my life. We might not have a lot of time for play, but that doesn't mean we shouldn't find ways to pursue it. Play means giving myself a break and rejuvenating. It's great when play can integrate with other dimensions, but that's not necessary. Play can mean simply watching a movie while traveling on a plane. That is very relaxing to me.

For me, play usually involves other people since I'm very social. It also means being open to new experiences. I can't resist when a friend asks me to go antiquing—to me, that's a release and it's fun. It could also mean going to the beach with my extended family and playing all day. For me, the ideal play is anything that gives me a sense of childlike wonder, and it doesn't necessarily need to have a specific intention. Just being open to something new and different is enough.

The words of Thich Nhat Hanh can help us understand the importance of play. In *The Art of Living,* he writes, "Aimlessness does not mean doing nothing. It means not putting something in front of you to chase after. When we remove the objects of our cravings and desires, we discover that happiness and freedom are available to us right here in the present moment." Electronic Arts CEO Andy Wilson has a pithy way of getting at what Thich Nhat Hanh is talking about, using his practice of Brazilian Jiu-Jitsu as an example: "When someone's trying to take your head off, you can pretty much only think about that."

If the best way you can save your head from the stresses of work and home is to risk having it kicked, I recommend you take it!

TAKEAWAYS

Carving out time for play is hard even once you reach the C-suite. But all is not lost. The essence of play itself is that it's a suspension of the pursuit of perfection. So let's stop pursuing perfection, and think instead of how we can restore ourselves through play. Here are some thoughts:

1. Consider play to be part of your self-care.

Most of us can't stop in the middle of a big meeting to do jumping jacks. But those of us who have integrated play into our lives have likely conditioned our minds to more easily downshift when things get tense. It is crucial that we be able to do so in heated moments when our adrenaline and cortisol threaten to take over. That's why I believe it is so important for people of all ages to cultivate their playful side. Having a mechanism to deescalate stressful situations and get out of our heads can be tremendously beneficial for our mental and physical well-being and our working relationships. Schedule playtime like you would important meetings, and protect that time.

2. Choose something you love.

Everyone should have at least one thing to which they look forward and to which they haven't assigned high expectations. If you want to become an expert at pottery, golf, or something else, fine. But picking something that gives you joy, release, and a sense of well-being is more important than becoming a pro.

3. Social or solitary? It's your choice.

When she was First Lady, Michelle Obama unwound by going on weekend getaways with her closest friends. In contrast, MSNBC journalist Rachel Maddow retreats to a country home and reads comic books. Know yourself and then consider whether you restore and energize yourself by being around others or by being alone.

4. Remember, it doesn't have to be a competition.

We are naturally competitive. But hopefully, we can derive enjoyment without making everything into a heated competition or exacting difficult standards and judgments on ourselves. Recreation ought to be our release, not another area in which we strive for perfection and which can deflate us if we fall short.

5. Encourage others to play.

If other people work for you, encourage them to take time out for play, whether it's board games, pickup basketball, or anything else that gets them out of themselves and the pressures of work. You will find they think more clearly and get more done. And, if you set a good example by taking time to play yourself, your employees will be more likely to do the same.

Chapter 4

GROWTH

"No one can take away what you know and learn; all other worldly possessions are accessible to others."

—ETABA

GROWTH OCCURS IN BOTH OUR PROFESSIONAL AND PERSONAL lives if we let it. It can come from intellectually stimulating pursuits that are not required for your career but that make you a fuller person. It can come from watching others at work and appreciating what they do and how they do it. It can come from reading books about new topics or from adding to your body of knowledge about a hobby or interest. You can grow by seeking advice from people you admire at your workplace or in your personal life. You can also grow by learning from mistakes and setbacks.

Growth can be boring and thankless at times. It means that we must do things to stretch our minds and put ourselves in uncomfortable situations for the sake of growth. I felt this way when my daughter was six years old and I was going to business school while working full time. Although I loved that environment of learning and camaraderie, I did not enjoy spending hours and hours reading case studies—hours I could have been spending with my daughter.

When we have a clear vision of what we want to achieve or be, we need to do things that may not directly apply to what we do today. We need to take time out of our busy lives to prepare for something that is not required for the job at hand. Such effort requires commitment and discipline. It is not easy to do. Throughout my career there have been clear tradeoffs, and I wanted to give up so many times. But I am glad I did not, as I have learned so much in the process.

Learning is essential to growth, but growth is not exclusively drawn from reading; it's about seeking enlightenment, being culturally engaged, and evolving our understanding of the world. When we identify our emotional triggers and work to dismantle them, that's growth. When we take on another's point of view, that's growth. When we stop taking others' behavior personally and recognize it as a reflection of where they are on their path in life, that's growth.

Growth requires us to find ways to open our eyes and discover a sense of spaciousness around our entrenched beliefs and understandings. We can apply this to all aspects of our life. Underpinning all growth is a mindset that allows it to happen, whether we pursue it proactively or look for it in the rubble of a setback.

Our deliberate choices to grow, or not to grow, affect our careers and the lives of loved ones and others who are part of our community. Just as all sides of a Rubik's Cube change when we turn just one side, whether we decide to grow also affects our health, our career, our self-care, and other realms for better or for worse. Growth can be temporarily painful and disruptive, but it usually is a risk well worth taking in the long term.

That's why we should want to evolve, especially in unexpected ways. When we test our boundaries, including professional ones, we realize that we can grow into an entirely different existence if we want to. That often comes at the price of giving up the self that we have become comfortable with or even attached to.

Not surprisingly, growth plays out quite differently for women than for men. While many women have to endure the stereotype that we become increasingly out of touch with the world around us as we age, women actually appear to have an advantage when it comes to growth. According to the leadership development consultancy Zenger/Folkman, women actually become more interested in self-improvement as they age, based on a study of more than seven thousand people.[60] This may be due to the fact that if we have been doing the work of getting to know ourselves, we become more self-aware over time, and we tend to become more confident as we age—at least compared to men.

The study's authors found that men's self-confidence increases until they hit their early forties. It dips for them in midlife and

60 Jack Zenger and Joseph Folkman, "How Age and Gender Affect Self-Improvement," *Harvard Business Review*, January 5, 2016, https://hbr.org/2016/01/how-age-and-gender-affect-self-improvement.

then rises until about age fifty-five, before it starts trending downward. Women's model for confidence is totally different. On average, we steadily increase in confidence from our mid-twenties until our mid-sixties; in the end, we are more confident than men.

The late, visual psychologist Rudolf Arnheim encouraged us to see aging not as an arch but rather as a staircase—a series of steady and constant opportunities for growth that present themselves over time, instead of dropping off after midlife as the arch metaphor would suggest. Actress Jane Fonda, who pointed to Arnheim's work in her 2011 book *Prime Time,* takes it a step further and suggests that the staircase can be a spiral, since wisdom does not come to us in a linear way.[61]

If women can grow in ways that make them more honest with themselves and with the people around them, it will not only help improve their leadership skills, but it will also help the companies that employ them. In other words, being authentic is a great personality trait. This is not wishful thinking. New research conducted by the Great Place to Work Institute reveals that the authenticity of leaders is a major factor in a business's success, and corporations are starting to get wise to this. When companies honor talented individuals for all that they are, without discriminating based on race, gender, or other typical prejudices, they are more inclusive. And as the institute discovered, inclusive companies experience up to three times the revenue growth of less-inclusive companies.

---

61 Jane Fonda, *Prime Time* (New York: Random House, 2011).

In terms of our discussion, I have found that growth and authenticity go hand in hand. In so many of the interviews I conducted, I realized that women recognized their growth the most when they also became aware of stepping into their most authentic self.

CHALLENGES TO GROWTH

The most popular phrase that touches on growth in many cultures is "growing pains." So many of us already have a deep-seated hesitation when it comes to matters of expansion. But, if tropes hold sway, let's focus on "no pain, no gain." Here are some of the pain points women contend with when it comes to growth, on and off the job.

We're afraid to ask for advice or help.

According to Chronus' "State of Women in the Workplace" report, 67 percent of women rate mentorship as highly important in career advancement, but 63 percent report that they've never had a mentor.[62] Chronus researchers found that this is largely due to women being hesitant to ask, for fear of being uncertain what response they will receive. For organizations with a formal mentorship program, half of all women had a mentor. In companies without a formal program, only one in four women said

---

62 "The State of Women in the Workplace," Chronus, 2018, https://get.chronus.com/CON-ModernMentoringWomeninWorkplace_ThankYou.html?aliId=eyJpIjoiWEhDQjA0UzlPYTMwSGs0QSIsInQiOiIyOU1RNHY2VmolT2RVM2NoRGtn-WHRBPT0ifQ%253D%253D.

they had a mentor. Another study, by the global management consulting and executive search firm Egon Zehnder, found that if women don't achieve a certain amount of success early enough in their career, they stop reaching out for support, or their organizations stop offering it to them.[63] The upshot: inadequate mentorship deprives women of professional growth.

Women feel the need to prove themselves rather than improve themselves.

The Zenger/Folkman study showed that women lose ground early in their careers because they feel they have to prove themselves, to a far greater degree than men. The authors point out that women are socialized to be less confident than men. This is likely an even bigger problem for women of color, who face more bias in the corporate world.

Growth can be time-consuming and difficult.

Learning new things and evolving is difficult, especially when we're taking on so much. Women, especially women of color, feel that they must spend so much energy overcompensating for discrimination in their companies, along with shouldering the burden of caring for others and running their homes. In this chapter, you'll read the story of Azalina Adham, former COO of Bursa Malaysia, which illustrates this point.

---

63 "Leaders & Daughters 2019 Global Survey," Egon Zehnder, 2019, https://www. egonzehnder.com/cdn/serve/article-pdf/1551458624-4d7443956c926957a5d8ddab-03be6676.pdf.

Sometimes growth doesn't feel good.

On the surface, growth seems inherently good, something all of us can embrace. We want those around us to believe we are growing. But in practice, it can mean drudgery and underappreciation, or on the other extreme, chaos and uncertainty. Women will face many long stretches during which they must find the value of growth and be their own cheerleaders. The story in this chapter about Sylvia Metayer—who is, fittingly, the Chief Growth Officer at Sodexo—illustrates this. And Amgen's Lori Johnston, whose own story illustrates how setbacks can spur the greatest growth, describes aspects of her growth as a "hot mess."

My own experience when I first came to the United States, trying to figure out what I wanted to do while earning a living by waiting on tables and bartending, is an excellent example of uncomfortable existence. It was not easy or fun, but a necessary step to get me to where I am today.

This is a perfect example of how growth in any dimension of our lives can fuel the other dimensions as well. Assessing my values and interests ultimately helped me in my first restaurant jobs. It led me to go to school to finish my undergraduate degree in business and, ten years later, to pursue an MBA at Temple University while working full time. In retrospect, I can see how all of that led me into the C-suite. It's like Steve Jobs said: "You can't connect the dots looking forward; you can only connect them looking backwards. So you have to trust that the dots will somehow connect in your future. You have to trust in something—your gut, destiny, life, karma, whatever."

I realized this when I returned to Cambridge, many years after I first arrived there, to enroll in the Advanced Management Program at Harvard Business School. When I'd go out to dinner at local restaurants with classmates, I'd remember my younger self, waiting tables and feeling in awe of the students who came to eat.

Sometimes we can't see our growth until we've achieved it and looked back down the hill to see where we started. For example, despite the pain of having my father taken from my family for so long and the difficult circumstances that came afterward, I am so grateful now for many of the lessons I learned from growing up in turbulent times in Ethiopia. They were more relevant to my career as a businesswoman than I ever could have imagined.

Lori Johnston, Executive Vice President and Chief Human Resources Officer at Amgen, best describes the path to achieving her full potential when she says, "There were days I was like a hot mess." When Lori was in college and juggling several jobs, she got pregnant, had her daughter, married, and had to put school on hold briefly. Then, just two weeks before graduation, she got divorced. "And then I stood up," she recalls. "I kept going. I brushed myself off. I'm prouder of that than I am of reaching the executive vice president level or anything. I'm really proud of the fact that I just got back up."

I see many women get caught up in the expectation—consciously or unconsciously—that progress is linear. But life is just too complicated for this to be true, as Lori's experiences show. She sees her ability to learn from setbacks as a gift.

Lori recalls getting interviewed for a magazine and being asked about her biggest failure. "I fail every day," she says, "and it's the little failures, to me, that have made the biggest difference in my life. It's the aspect of falling down, getting up, brushing myself off, and going back in. And that allows you to be open to feedback; it allows you to be transparent with yourself. It allows you to be honest."

When men made mistakes, Lori would watch with interest at how they'd respond to it. "Even in a meeting they'd say something that was really stupid, and then they would just shrug it off and go on," she says. "And I thought, 'You know what? We say something stupid, and we're thinking about it four years later.' We could talk about the temperature of the room where everybody was, what happened, how we felt, what we said, what we should have said. Men don't even care because I think they learn early that you just shake it off and go on. You don't worry about it."

Unfortunately, most women are not like that. We agonize over our failures much longer than we celebrate our successes. In my own case, sometimes it is not even a failure, but the *perception* of one, that I agonize over. I may be in a meeting where I thought I messed up or my message was not received as intended. In the past, I've spent hours analyzing what happened, to the point that it took time and focus away from other important things. Now I ask for feedback from others immediately after the event so I can get a more objective perspective, learn from them, and do things differently next time.

Today I often tell my mentees, "People in the meeting are often focused on themselves. They are not as focused on you as you think they are." In any situation, if you present yourself as some-one who is there to help and move the conversation forward, you won't need to dwell on how others perceive you.

Understanding how to turn our missteps into renewal and growth opportunities helps us own and value our failures, rather than fear them.

Our growth as women in the corporate world certainly can improve with the help of mentors. But this, too, is a dicey prop-osition for women. A story from the life of Lorna Donatone, the former CEO of Geographic Regions for Sodexo, illustrates this well. She says, "I graduated from grad school in 1982. I thought the key to my future was keeping my head down and working hard. It was, but [in] retrospect, it was about much more, too. I wish I had picked up my head a few times and looked around for a mentor. Back then, formal mentoring programs were rare, but informal mentoring has been happening since the begin-ning of time. I wish I had sought that out, especially among the female leaders with whom I crossed paths, because I now see that mentoring can give us a safe place to ask for advice and help. It can provide the wisdom of someone who has faced the chal-lenges in front of us, or has more experience with the landscape, or just has a different point of view."

Andi Owen, President and CEO of Herman Miller, has a very interesting take on the feedback dilemma. Her early experiences helped train her to seek out criticism, even when it was difficult to hear. During her time in the art world, she says, critiques were a part of life, whether for auditions, poetry, essays, or visual art.

She became accustomed from an early age to receiving a lot of constructive criticism, which she feels gave her an appreciation for it that others may not share.

"I learned which constructive feedback to use and which feedback to let go of because I did not agree with it," says Andi. "That was a valuable skill to have in the business world. For most of my career I worked for men, with the occasional exception. I have found that men have been much less willing to give women feedback than to give other men feedback, so I have always had to be very aggressive in seeking it out."

But Andi, tenacious as she is, wishes she had had more confidence when she was younger. She says, "If I had been more confident, I probably would have been faster to get things done and would have probably been more successful earlier on. But at the same time, I look back and my experiences are what make me who I am today, so I look at them differently now." She believes that she ended up exactly where she wanted to be—that it all worked out.

Andi also shared with me that her inspiration to grow came not from a wise old mentor but her fifteen-year-old son. "As far as giving meaning to my life and making me a better person, being plugged into what's going on inside my son's brain and understanding what's important to him, how he is using technology and interacting with people, getting to see what his world is like and how different it is from mine—that really keeps me current when I think about the problems we deal with in the corporate environment," says Andi.

She adds that having a teenager has helped make her more aware of the potential of new technologies and more comfortable communicating with younger colleagues. "We've got five generations in the workforce now and they couldn't be more different from each other," Andi says, "so the advantage I have with a youngster at home is just mind-opening. I know all the latest apps and songs and games, and I know how to communicate, and I know what young people are thinking about, what's important to them as a population." Being keyed into her son's generation also enables her to bring new ideas to the table.

I noticed a correlation between Andi's enthusiasm for learning from her son and the very refreshing and beginner's mind she brings to her role as CEO. For example, she told me, "I love going down to the design yard where we have a lot of collaboration with outside designers, and I spend time listening to how they think, how they solve problems, how the engineers think about the design of the chair." She says that's one of the most fun parts of her job.

"When you consider customers," says Andi, "you have to inherently be thinking about the future—how people live, how people work, the forces that change the way they behave. I try to anticipate what's coming. Those conversations and the amount of research we do in my current role are really enlightening."

Andi says that Herman Miller bases its whole philosophy on how people work best. "How are they most productive? What kinds of environments do people want to work in? I don't have an office or a desk. My work life is so much more enriching and productive, as I'm able to see people in the organization."

She says that kind of contact is one of the best parts of her job because it enables her to learn something new from her colleagues every day. "I don't feel like 'the expert.' I'm new to this industry and am always asking 'why.' I love constantly learning, especially in this job. Typically, at the CEO level you're seen as the 'expert.' I'm the inverse of that." She adds that while she may be talented from a leadership or talent-development standpoint, she is still "learning the business," even at this advanced stage of her career.

Like Andi, several other women I interviewed told me their growth was inspired by their children's approach to learning and life. Growth is not synonymous with the pursuit of perfection. In fact, the pressure we put on ourselves to be perfect inhibits our authentic growth. Lori Johnston tells me, "One of my daughters was a perfectionist and she pushed herself and took this really hard course at school. She got a C on one test. And I told her, 'I am putting that on the refrigerator. Girl, I am more proud of this grade than any grade you've had, because you've pushed yourself out there. This C is something you should be proud of. And I'm displaying it.' We've got to teach that to our girls."

Lori relates something she told her daughter, which I think is really true: "It's the art of picking back up and then saying, 'What do I do with it?' I call it 'fail fast, fail hard, fail early.' That stuff to me is more valuable than anything else. I'm proud of the fact that I got up."

When we stop putting pressure on ourselves to force particular outcomes, real growth can emerge. This was confirmed for me by Gerri Mason Hall, the Chief Diversity and Social Responsibility

Officer for Sodexo. As her career has advanced, Gerri has tried not to focus as much on particular goals. "I am not so milestone-driven anymore," she says. "That might have driven me to get married and have a child too early because I was looking at milestones. I saw my path vertically—starting with my undergrad degree; then my juris doctorate; then I looked to what was next. Now I have to reflect on what my life's mission or purpose might be."

Gerri's comment reaffirms the need to anchor our milestones with purpose and values. Whenever you set a milestone ask "why?" five times to ensure that your milestones are aligned with your purpose and values. I think Gerri is going to succeed brilliantly at this because she exhibits a wonderful interest in growth.

She told me, "When I'm not working, I love gaining knowledge." And that's not just through enrolling in master classes. One of Gerri's favorite outlets is watching the television program *The Henry Ford Innovation Nation,* hosted by Mo Rocca, which offers episodes on everything from the science behind hospital robots to interviews with innovative entrepreneurs like Ali Webb, the founder of Drybar. "I love things that teach me something new," she says, "even something as simple as a cooking show that teaches me to substitute one ingredient for another."

But growing and evolving can be difficult because growth often comes out of pain and hardship. Azalina Adham first attended school in Malaysia and continued her education in the United States. In Asia, gentleness and niceness were prized attributes in female students. These qualities served her well—until she began school stateside. She was afraid to speak her mind in class, especially when brash boys were commanding the room. She remembers being bullied and forced to make most of the contributions to group work. "By the time I finished my senior year, I could handle that," says Azalina. "I think I got a lot tougher in the US." Even though Azalina became proud of her ability to speak up for herself, she realized that she needed to refine her approach into something that was authoritative rather than overly tough.

"My parents never inhibited us from speaking our minds," says Azalina. "I still do that today. If there's something that's not right, I'll say so. Otherwise I'll be very uncomfortable. But I had to learn to harness it a bit, to express [my objection] in a way that was not so offensive and say what I wanted to say more tactfully. I didn't change my values or my views, but the way I would deliver my message [made it] more palatable for someone to listen to my viewpoint."

As with Azalina, Azita Shariati's early experiences helped fuel her growth and shape her approach to dealing with others. "The Iranian Revolution took place when I was eleven, and they decided to close all the private schools," recalled Azita, Group CEO of AniCura. "This was one of the biggest changes in my life. I went from coed classes at a Jewish private school to a public girls-only school, since the Muslim religion did not permit coed schools. All the friendships I had made were destroyed because most of the Jewish people left Iran after the revolution. There was no direct impact on my family; however, most of my network of friends was gone and I had to create a whole new [one]. It was difficult in the beginning. When people [found out] I came from [a] private school, they did not relate to me initially. After a while, they opened up to me. I was always thinking about them and trying to be part of [the group]."

These early experiences taught her to empathize with others, which serves her well today. "From my schooling, I learned a lot about inclusion and how to create a common platform," she notes.

As Azita's experience shows, sometimes growth can be arduous and lonely. Sylvia Metayer, Chief Growth Officer at Sodexo, recalled the strange experience from early in her career of getting hired by a company that accidentally filled her position before she got there. While she was still brought on board, she had no idea what to do with herself and was given little direction. This forced her to open her horizons and innovate ways she could make herself indispensable to the company—even without a job title!

"When people ask me for tips on jobs, I say, 'I did everything,'" says Sylvia. "There is always something in an office that needs to get done, right? So I thought, well, I'll make it so great that they have an extra pair of hands. I did everything. I did the most boring things. Anything—well, almost anything, except the filing. And I would have done the filing, except it would have made the assistants and the typists uncomfortable for their jobs. I became indispensable, and I got the attention of somebody who was fairly high up in the organization, who gave me a promotion."

Companies and cultures can overlook or undervalue the need for growth, which Sylvia also knows all too well. A Frenchwoman born in Eritrea, she has lived in Canada, the United States, and France and feels she became a more well-rounded and open-minded leader by working in several countries. But moving around also impacted her earnings potential. She says, "At many companies, they only recognized what you knew through that company; it's like nothing you've done outside of their company is really of interest to them."

Still, even when others couldn't appreciate Sylvia's growth, she found value in it. "In the US, the Americans didn't always understand what I was worth, what I could do," Sylvia says. "It helped me be a better manager and a better leader, because I could very quickly understand the capability of others. And later, I felt as though I could understand what it was like to be an American affiliate of a French company. I felt as though I knew what people meant when they were talking. It's not just a question of language—I speak several languages—but of culture."

Not all growth, incidentally, is right for us, as one of Lorna Donatone's reminiscences about her career trajectory reveals. "There was a time when I wondered whether my whole career would be about repair and fix, sales and bankruptcy," recalls Lorna. "If that was a skillset I was developing, I wasn't sure it was [one] I wanted to have." Being in touch with our values helps us grow in the right direction, which makes setting aside time for reflection so important. However, what I also realize is that very few of us are taught how to reflect well. If we don't know our values, how can we possibly make decisions that are aligned with them?

While many of us might not have had official mentors, I think most of us can come up with at least a short list of people who have been like guardian angels, who are more experienced than us, who care about our well-being, and whom we admire enough to seek out their advice. The process of listing such people is adapted from a grounding technique promoted by executive coach Vasavi Kumar, who works with highly driven entrepreneurs. It is a great way to start getting clear on what matters most to us. These mentor figures don't even need to be physically present for this exercise.

First, make a short list of the people you admire the most and take note of why you admire each of them. When you have a situation in your life that you just can't seem to get clarity on, conjure up this list. Of course, it's most ideal if you can talk to them in person, or by phone or videoconferencing. But you can also imagine conversations with them. State your dilemma as honestly as possible to them and request their feedback. If possible, ask two or more people for their take on the situation. You are likely to find that while you may admire your cohort equally, they may have contradictory ideas on what you should be doing. And that's okay—in fact, it's welcome!

This process takes time. But if you are vulnerable and if you are comfortable confronting difficult options, you will likely gain a greater sense of who you are and what you want. And, as Kumar says, over time you will internalize this skill and your newfound understanding of yourself and become your own reliable point of reference.

A wise adage says that we get what we give. In that spirit, we might all do well to seek opportunities to foster the growth of others, particularly women coming up in the ranks behind us or women we see struggling. By devoting our time and talents in situations where they can be received graciously, we help advance the interests of women everywhere and inadvertently end up bringing more blessings upon ourselves.

Whatever we give our attention to has the potential to grow. Let's make sure we are putting positive solutions into the world by helping to create them for ourselves and others. Lori Johnston wisely gets at the heart of how we can all help one another when she advises men to seek out dialogues with working women. "I would say to men, 'Spend time talking to a woman about what it takes to be a woman executive. Listen and be a part of creating [an] environment where women can succeed.'"

Lori counsels her female peers to temper their competitive drive with a helpful spirit. "[Having] so few positions at the top... creates competition," she says. "We're competitive just by virtue of the fact that we've gotten through life, and so we're scrappy and competitive. You almost have to consciously switch that orientation so that you can look around and help a person next to you."

TAKEAWAYS

Now that we have gathered some strength and inspiration from women who have committed to growth—and have seen its benefits in their lives—let's consider some of the action steps.

1. Embrace your authentic self.

You can't grow by stifling yourself. You can't grow by hiding or suppressing. You have to break free of the trappings of the person you thought you were and embrace who you are and what you can be. If you are not authentic, you are acting, and even the best of us can only keep up the act for so long. Even if you are an expert at keeping up the façade, who wants to be typecast?

2. Rethink "milestones."

Growth is a continuous process, different from pursuing a degree or achieving a certain level in your career.

3. Fail fast, fail hard, fail early.

As Lori Johnston points out, failures build resilience, which will make you more confident taking risks in the name of personal growth. She was wise to celebrate her young daughter's C grade in a challenging subject at school, knowing that falling short of a goal can trigger growth.

4. See a staircase, not an arch.

As Rudolf Arnheim pointed out, aging brings constant opportunities for wisdom and growth and should be seen as a staircase— not an arch along which we "peak" then decline.

5. Stretch your capabilities.

I challenge myself to learn something new every day, whether that's formally by taking a class or casually as in reading historical fiction with my monthly book club, where we often read books on subjects I might not otherwise study. Learning helps us comprehend a complex world. Given that the world is ever more complex, learning should never end. As Einstein once put it, "Intellectual growth should commence at birth and cease only at death."

6. Set aside time for self-reflection.

Reflection must be practiced regularly. There is no one right way to do this; find a way that works for you, but make time for self-reflection and make it part of your daily routine.

7. Look for opportunities to encourage growth in other women.

Emma Lazarus, author of the words cast in bronze on the Statue of Liberty, also wrote this: "Until we are all free, we are none of us free." Let's help each other find the freedom that living up to our fullest potential can bring. Our growth is in vain if it comes at the expense of others.

Chapter 5

SELF-CARE

"When you take care of yourself, you have taken care of all others."

—ETABA

THE NEW YORK TIMES REPORTS THAT THE LATE BRENDA Barnes "sparked a national debate about women juggling career and family" when she famously stepped down from her position as the Pepsi-Cola North America CEO in 1997, to spend more time with her children. "There were two things in my life, kids and job," Barnes told a reporter. "Exercise? Golf? Sleep? None of that."

Even though Barnes was a wealthy and successful executive at the time, she admitted that she had little time to do things for herself. In an interview with *The Christian Science Monitor* she gave after leaving Pepsi-Cola, Barnes said balancing work and family required that she wake up every day at 3:30 a.m. "You end up making choices, and what's not all that important you just eliminate," she said. "So you cut back on your sleep and on things for yourself. If you want to play tennis and go to the beauty salon and go shopping, then you probably can't have three kids and have the kind of job I have."[64]

Like Barnes, who died of complications from a stroke in 2017, too many of us striving for the C-suite—especially women of color and those with limited money or time—tend to put the proverbial oxygen mask on others before putting on our own. We focus on our colleagues, our kids, our partners, and our parents while shortchanging ourselves. Unlike Barnes, who was self-aware enough to step back when she realized she couldn't handle it all, many of us don't realize how little oxygen we are giving ourselves. Caring for ourselves must be a much higher priority if we're to get to the tops of organizations and have a full life outside of them. But what does self-care really mean?

Self-care is vital to our physical and mental health. Healthcare professionals agree on the basics: a healthy diet, physical activity, good hygiene, adequate sleep, medical and mental healthcare, and stress reduction. But self-care is also a very personal dimension, with other facets based on what the individual needs to feel at her best. For some, it might entail attention to appearance, regular massages, time with a loved one who nurtures and restores us, a hobby, or a small pleasure that revitalizes us. Along with regular doctor visits, mental healthcare if needed, sleep, movement, and diet, every woman must also be in touch with those other aspects that compose her unique view of self-care. Then, she must make self-care a priority.

---

64 Shelley Donald Coolidge, "Trading 30,000 Staff For 3 Kids," *The Christian Science Monitor*, October 8, 1997, https://www.csmonitor.com/1997/1008/100897. econ.econ.1.html.

WHY IT'S NECESSARY

Ashley Whillans, a Harvard Business School professor who studies the correlation between how women spend their time and their level of contentment, shared some interesting insights on the *Women at Work* podcast. She said, "When I think about self-care, I think about really the predictors of happiness. Do I have enough time to spend with people that I care about? What is the quality of my social interactions? Do I feel like I have control over my time, over my schedule, over the tasks that I'm completing? And do I feel optimistic about where my life is going?"[65] Self-care is important because it enables us to answer "yes" to those questions.

Self-care wards off stress.

The debilitating effects of chronic stress are real dangers to women in the C-suite. The American Psychological Association (APA) says chronic stress often leads to "catastrophizing"— making the problems in our lives seem more burdensome than they are—because we don't make time to check ourselves and put problems in perspective. Emotional stress "can trigger heart attacks, arrhythmias, and even sudden death," the APA notes.[66] Even worse, heart conditions often sneak up and catch the overstressed worker by surprise.

---

65 "Women at Work," *Harvard Business Review,* April 20, 2020, https://hbr.org/podcast/2020/04/making-the-most-of-this-mess.

66 "How stress affects your health," American Psychological Association, 2013, https://www.apa.org/topics/stress-health.

Self-care helps us do our jobs better.

As Whillans points out, employees whose supervisors give them leeway to balance work and family time report they are 40 percent more focused on the job.[67]

Women of color face additional health problems; self-care can mitigate some of them.

According to the US Census Bureau's February 2020 "Population Estimates and Projections," the expected lifespan for Black women trails that of white women by more than three years.[68] Racism, unequal access to the components of healthy living, and other societal problems explain much of it. In a study of 223 Black women, published online by the National Library of Medicine in 2019, professors from University of California-Los Angeles and Morgan State University in Baltimore found that self-care can mitigate the stress that imperils Black women's health. Their research cited studies linking Black women's stress and concluded: "Discrimination is a key factor contributing to poor mental health and self-reported health (SRH) over time, with poor SRH as a key predictor of morbidity and

---

67 "Women at Work," *Harvard Business Review,* November 11, 2019, https://hbr.org/podcast/2019/11/how-we-take-care-of-ourselves

68 Lauren Medina, Shannon Sabo, and Jonathan Vespa, "Living Longer: Historical and Projected Life Expectancy in the United States, 1960 to 2060," US Census Bureau, February 2020, https://www.census.gov/content/dam/Census/library/publications/2020/demo/p25-1145.pdf.

mortality."[69] While the ideal solution is to address and correct these inequities, women of color must be especially intentional about their self-care in the meantime.

Congresswoman Alexandria Ocasio-Cortez, a Latina and a style icon, sees self-care as a way for women to defy cultural definitions of beauty. In a YouTube video of her putting on makeup—watched more than three million times—Ocasio-Cortez declares that her beauty regimen is a form of empowerment: "Our culture is so predicated on diminishing women and preying on our self-esteem," she says. "It's quite a radical act and a mini-protest to love yourself in a society that tells you you're not the right weight and not the right color. You can stand up and say, 'you don't make that decision; I make that decision.'"[70]

CHALLENGES TO SELF-CARE

When we are conscious of the limitations in our lives, we can stop framing them as reasons not to take care of ourselves and instead find ways to transcend them. Ours is a world where time is money, and women in particular encounter so many barriers to taking care of themselves. To that end, here are some common struggles many of us would do well to remediate.

---

69 Paris B Adkins-Jackson, Jocelyn Turner-Musa, and Charlene Chester, "The Path to Better Health for Black Women: Predicting Self-Care and Exploring Its Mediating Effects on Stress and Health," University of California and Morgan State University, September 5, 2019, https://pubmed.ncbi.nlm.nih.gov/31486346.

70 "Congresswoman Alexandria Ocasio-Cortez's Guide to Her Signature Red Lip | Beauty Secrets | Vogue," *Vogue,* August 21, 2020, https://www.youtube.com/watch?v=bXqZllqGWGQ&feature=youtu.be.

We're stretched too thin.

PayScale research has found that women with the same job title and qualifications as a man would need to work more than a year longer than he would to earn the same amount of money.[71] Who really wants to take time for herself when she is already feeling behind and overwhelmed?

Oxford Economics found that in 2018 Americans left 768 million vacation days unused, and 236 million of them were forfeited completely, totaling $65.5 billion in lost benefits.[72] The top three reasons reported for giving up vacation days were: employees were concerned about looking replaceable, they considered their workload too heavy, and they lacked coverage at work. It's no surprise, then, that so many of the women I interviewed felt that the self-care dimension was unbalanced in their lives.

In a 2018 study of 1,000 women by CGI Health, HealthyWomen, and *Redbook* magazine, nearly half said they neglected their health because they didn't have time to focus on it.[73] And quite a number of us, especially women who work in corporations, lead a very sedentary existence, fixed at our desk in front of our

---

71 "The State Of The Gender Pay Gap In 2020," PayScale, 2020, https://www.payscale.com/data/gender-pay-gap.

72 "Study: A Record 768 Million U.S. Vacation Days Went Unused in '18, Opportunity Cost in the Billions," Oxford Economics, US Travel Association, and Ipsos, August 16, 2019, https://www.ustravel.org/press/study-record-768-million-us-vacation-days-went-unused-18-opportunity-cost-billions#:~:text=American%20workers%20left%20a%20record,%2465.5%20billion%20in%20lost%20benefits.

73 "Up to 50% of Women Neglecting Their Own Health," GCI Health, HealthyWomen, and *Redbook* Magazine, April 20, 2018, https://gcihealth.com/article/up-to-50-of-women-neglecting-their-own-health.

computers, glancing at our smartphones, trying to keep up with our inbox as we shuttle from one meeting to another, from one conference room to another, from plane to train to car. And so, self-care gets pushed farther and farther down on our to-do lists until it gets pushed off altogether because we run out of time.

Our companies don't encourage self-care.

A study conducted by HealthFitness, a firm of expert wellness-culture builders, found that more than half of full-time employees of companies that offer a health, wellness, and fitness program decline to participate, despite their desire to be healthier, because of an unsupportive company culture or concerns about workplace privacy. HealthFitness concluded that, "Everyone from the CEO to individual managers need[s] to explicitly tell their employees that it's OK to take a break during the day to use the gym, go for a walk, or attend an aerobics class—and it's important that these facilities and activities are readily accessible."[74] Many of the women I spoke with excelled at being good role models for others; the work they put into self-care and fitness, however, often required them to renew their commitment to themselves.

Women of color face additional difficulties.

Black women represent 6.5 percent of the American population but suffer the highest incidences of heart disease, cancer, stroke,

---

74 Sean McManamy, "Why People Do—and Don't—Participate in Wellness Programs," *Harvard Business Review*, October 10, 2016, https://hbr.org/2016/10/why-people-do-and-dont-participate-in-wellness-programs.

and diabetes, the National Institutes of Health pointed out in a 2017 report.[75] The Centers for Disease Control and Prevention estimate that 56 percent of Black women aged twenty and older are obese.[76]

A study of more than six hundred Black women, published in 2017 in the journal *Counseling Psychology*, found that awareness of others' stereotypes about them tended to make the women feel anxious, depressed, and angry; less likely to care for themselves; and possibly more likely to turn to drugs and alcohol.[77] A 2018 report by Catalyst pointed out that 58 percent of Black women professionals feel "highly on guard" at work because they anticipate being singled out or excluded because of their race.[78] More than half of those who felt guarded said they had trouble sleeping as a result. The UCLA/Morgan State study I referenced earlier in this chapter echoed these findings.[79]

---

75 "Women of Color Health Data Book," National Institutes of Health, 2017, https://orwh.od.nih.gov/sites/orwh/files/docs/WoC-Databook-FINAL.pdf.

76 "Health of Black or African American non-Hispanic Population," Centers for Disease Control and Prevention, last reviewed May 7, 2021, https://www.cdc.gov/nchs/fastats/black-health.htm.

77 M. C. Jerald, E. R. Cole, L. M. Ward, and L. R. Avery, "Controlling images: How awareness of group stereotypes affects Black women's well-being," *Journal of Counseling Psychology*, 2017, https://psycnet.apa.org/doiLanding?doi=10.1037%2Fcou0000233.

78 Dnika J. Travis and Jennifer Thorpe-Moscon, "Day-to-Day Experiences of Emotional Tax Among Women and Men of Color in the Workplace," Catalyst, February 15, 2018, https://www.catalyst.org/research/day-to-day-experiences-of-emotional-tax-among-women-and-men-of-color-in-the-workplace.

79 Paris B. Adkins-Jackson, Jocelyn Turner-Musa, and Charlene Chester, "The Path to Better Health for Black Women: Predicting Self-Care and Exploring Its Mediating Effects on Stress and Health," University of California and Morgan State University, September 5, 2019, https://pubmed.ncbi.nlm.nih.gov/31486346.

Women of color also struggle with long-engrained societal expectations. They are expected, demanded even, to be resilient. The stereotype of the "strong Black woman" is the standard to which many in society hold women of color. In her research on this topic, Dr. Jasmine Abrams, Assistant Professor of Psychology at the University of Maryland, Baltimore County, found that many Black women who see themselves as strong were inspired by their mothers, aunts, grandmothers, and other older role models who held it all together in the face of turmoil.[80] Abrams points to evidence that this stereotype has existed since the days of slavery, based on how Black women would console loved ones when families were ripped apart.

Striving to always be seen as strong and resilient impacts women's health, Dr. Cheryl Woods-Giscombé found in her study published in 2010. "The women surveyed routinely worked late, neglected taking breaks, sacrificed sleep, and put their health in danger to reach their goals," she notes.[81] The archetypal "strong Black woman" also carries the stress of others in an effect called "Network Stress."

Busy, ambitious women often struggle to take enough time for themselves, and many will admit they rarely put themselves first. However, those who have prioritized self-care, in ways that range from no-cost to extravagant, say it has become an important component of their well-being.

---

80   Jasmine A. Abrams, Ashley Hill, and Morgan Maxwell, "Underneath the Mask of the Strong Black Woman Schema: Disentangling Influences of Strength and Self-Silencing on Depressive Symptoms among U.S. Black Women," Sex Roles, 2019, https://link.springer.com/article/10.1007/s11199-018-0956-y.

81   Cheryl Woods-Giscombé, "Superwoman Schema: African American Women's Views on Stress, Strength, and Health," Qualitative Health Research, May 2010, https://www.ncbi.nlm.nih.gov/pmc/articles/PMC3072704/#_ffn_sectitle.

Lorna Donatone, former CEO of Geographic Regions for Sodexo, says, "I think we overachieve, and many of us ha[ve] to do that to be equal with our male counterparts. We ha[ve] to be three times as good." However, over the years she has learned that you shouldn't "sacrifice yourself for your work." When her agenda was full of international business travel, Lorna did not have the luxury of working out in just one place, but she found a mode of exercise—CrossFit—that she enjoyed and could pursue in gyms around the globe. "I was in the South of France a few years ago and I sought out a gym. The session was all in French, but I knew what they were talking about." Lorna aimed to retire "in the best shape, not the worst shape."

What a powerful act of self-validation! Lorna recognizes that she is worth self-care, no matter what stage of life she is in. She is not basing her worth on her career achievements; she knows she will still be valuable in the next phase of her life.

Tracey Gray-Walker, the CEO of American Veterinary Medical Association (AVMA) Trusts and the mother of an adult son with autism, says she still finds it challenging to find time for herself despite her success. "I don't think we give enough time to caring for ourselves," she says. "And I really think that we put everyone else in front of us. I'm always thinking about my son. I'm thinking about my husband. I'm thinking about work. But I don't put myself in the number one, two, or three slot. I've heard it many times: 'You know, Mommy can't be all she could be for other people if she's not everything she needs to be for herself.' So conceptually, you get it. But do I really apply it? No, I don't."

Gerri Mason Hall takes a holistic approach to self-care. She pays particular attention to grooming, nutrition, and exercise. She tells me with a laugh that one of her sisters couldn't be more different than her in this way: "She will not get a pedicure; she doesn't like people touching her. I appreciate the power of touch. I will get a massage or facial because that's part of me. The grooming is less about looks for me; it's how I feel in the process as well. When I get my hair cut, I feel good during the process."

It was especially heartening to hear how many women undertook their rituals for their own pleasure rather than to improve how they look to others. It seems that as we age, we become much better attuned to our own inner voice and needs and less worried about trying to impress everyone else. I believe that when we flourish in all seven dimensions, taking care of ourselves is a part of nurturing ourselves. We realize that we don't need to devote our time to putting on a facade for others.

Flavia Bittencourt, now Adidas' General Manager for Brazil, learned through her previous role as a Sephora top executive that making time for beauty does not have to be a superficial pursuit. Like Alexandria Ocasio-Cortez, Bittencourt sees self-care as a key to confidence and assertiveness. "Women especially need time for themselves to go to the salon and the like," she says. "Otherwise, we don't like what we see when we look in the mirror. For me, that's especially true now that I work in beauty. If a woman doesn't feel good with her image, she won't feel confident enough in a meeting, with friends, or in her relationships or romantic prospects. At Sephora the beauty makeover is important in making a woman feel incredible. I have seen this firsthand. It's not solely about beauty; it is about feeling good and liking yourself."

Bongiwe Ntuli, CFO and Executive Director of The Foschini Group, wishes she could have told her younger self that neglected health really catches up with you in your forties. "I wish I practiced self-care more than I do," she says. "I used to go every month to a spa for massages, facials, etc. Now that I'm in my forties, I have learned that health is not just about going to a health spa periodically; it's also important to eat well and go to the gym regularly. Health is an everyday, conscious decision."

These days Bongiwe works out for thirty minutes most days a week, a practice that helped her lose more than twenty pounds. She is in touch with how she feels physically and mentally and recalibrates her habits to get back on track if needed. "A few years back, I drank too much alcohol as I went out almost every evening, without knowing the damage I was causing myself," she says. "These bad social habits made me sleep poorly and I felt tired all the time. When I reduced alcohol significantly and increased my exercise, I felt a whole lot better, and had much more energy in the mornings."

Like Bongiwe, Karen Brown also has learned to tend to the basics of self-care. Karen, Founder and Managing Director of Bridge Arrow, a diversity consulting firm, got by on four hours of sleep a night when she was working her way up in the corporate world, before she struck out on her own. She says she would read about accomplished people who bragged about needing little sleep and thought it was a badge of honor. Her work responsibilities would dominate her thoughts in the wee hours of the morning, keeping her awake.

Finally, she realized this wasn't healthy and visited a sleep doctor.

"I had to get a doctor's help to help me understand what is best for me," says Karen. "And so, through the help of that sleep doctor, I learned how to sleep again. This is something that I do not compromise anymore." Karen also improves her sleep through daily exercise and bubble baths when she is especially stressed.

Along with taking care of herself physically, Bongiwe has some wise advice for women of all financial circumstances: your inner beauty shows on the outside, too. "Self-confidence and inner beauty cost nothing," she says. "Doing something good for someone, in any small way, shows outwardly—and makes you look at life differently and creates 'good air' about you, which is attractive!"

Lori Johnston, Executive Vice President and Chief Human Resources Officer of Amgen, spent a good chunk of her earliest years putting others' needs ahead of her own. Lori went to work full time at the age of fourteen to help her parents, who struggled financially due to her father's health problems. She graduated from college as a newly divorced, single mother and dove head-first into a demanding and exhilarating career, starting at Dell Computer when it was just a startup.

Early in her career, Lori would have felt guilty taking time to herself. Her own health epiphany came about fifteen years ago, when she had an episode at work that was eerily similar to the one that had claimed her beloved thirty-seven-year-old sister's life a few years earlier. "At Amgen, we had these patios outside the executive's office," she recalls. "I was in a meeting there with my supervisor. I looked at him, and I said, 'Something is wrong with my heart, and I think I'm going to go down.' My heart was racing, and you can feel that feeling when you're about to black out. I said, 'I need you to tell my family that I love them dearly,' and I passed out." Lori went into the hospital and was diagnosed with atrial fibrillation. She underwent a cauterization procedure, which fixed the issue. She says she realized then the importance of preventative care—that you have to take care of your health starting as early as possible.

Today, Lori is much better at paying attention to what she needs. She says that her self-care regimen restores her and gives her the energy to tackle her job and maintain the most important relationships in her life. Her biggest indulgence, she says, is getting up at 5 a.m. to spend two hours in her bathroom suite to read, text friends, and pamper herself before heading out to a day that she describes as "packed with meetings, meetings, meetings." Along with this "extravagance," she also has no-cost self-care routines, including carving out quiet time to decompress at the end of a long day. A self-identified introvert, Lori says her cooldown time is sacred to her. "I don't feel the need to go out and be with people," she says. "I spend a lot of time on the weekends recharging at home. I find the most relaxing things are going on hikes with my husband and doing things like that."

Like Lori, Debbie White sees self-care as carving out time for herself, rather than pampering herself at a salon. "My sisters-in-law and others in my family say I don't spend enough time on self-care," says Debbie, who has served as an executive at several companies, including Sodexo. "I think that what's more important is creating space for things, whether that's reflection, or getting a manicure, or spending time with family. When I was commuting from London to the US for work, those seven hours on the plane were really useful times for me because it really allowed me to reflect without any interruption of phone, emails, or whatever."

As Lori and Debbie demonstrate, spa visits, vacation getaways, dinners out, and expensive gifts may provide nice immediate comforts, but self-care doesn't need to be an extravagance. What is most sustaining—and substantive—is regularly making time for ourselves, unfettered and without distraction. And we have to prioritize it, hoard it, guard it, make sure it doesn't fall off our list of things to do.

Even when she was an international sales executive for DuPont Corp. with young children at home, consultant Maria Boulden prioritized self-care but loved the challenge of achieving it without spending much—a habit inherited from Depression-era parents who raised their children to be fiscally conservative but not cheap. She found a ninety-minute reflexology massage in Kuala Lampur for 100 ringgits and a two-hour massage with a pedicure in Shanghai for 150 RMB (both around US$25). She would occasionally splurge, but only on experiences that nurture all the senses, like dinner at her favorite Lebanese restaurant at the base of the Burj Kahlifa in Dubai to watch the fountain show. Her biggest treat is buying herself a new pair of running shoes and what she calls "pampering [her]self with time." Maria's self-care priorities include a disciplined diet, early morning runs (because there's nothing like touring a city as it's waking up), and watching American football or going to the beach with her husband and grown children.

Maria says the exercise and quiet time help her perform better on the job. "There's a physicality to this work," she explains. "We work crazy hours, and lots of them, while crossing multiple time zones each week. It's like you have to train for the job. And if you're out of shape, not just in body but in mind and spirit, it's going to get to you. I have colleagues whose lives have completely unraveled (or been lost) because of stress. Exercise is like a catharsis for me. I feel like if I can overcome the mental aspects of that physical challenge, there's nothing that day's gonna throw at me that I can't do."

A busy global-travel schedule has never kept Maria from her running regimen; she researches the safest neighborhoods in her destination city and always packs her running shoes. And when she is home, Maria most enjoys just being "present" and soaking up every moment with family. "I love having unstructured time to savor things," she says.

Like Maria, Andi Owen also believes in the importance of exercise and downtime. She says, "I try to find a way to do that almost every day. Even if it's a small amount of time, it's a time for me—emotionally cleansing and stress reducing."

Sharing downtime with loved ones is a form of self-care. Andi insists that when she is home, her family must sit down to eat together for dinner. "I'm a really strong believer in having that time to be together and just talk," Andi says. "Now that my son has gotten older, we allow him one night a week to have dinner with his friends."

Andi adds that it's important to be fully present during times with loved ones, rather than preoccupied with work and just going through the motions. "We have a multigenerational household, so my mother and I garden together, and my husband and I love to ride our bikes and go on surfing vacations when we can get time off. Spending time with family is paramount."

Lorna Donatone no longer reads business or self-help books as she did when she was younger, a great recognition of her own inner resources. While she once found the books interesting and entertaining, she has learned to trust her own voice and that of close friends and family. Instead of putting that pressure on herself, she will instead read for pleasure on her Kindle, or play games like Scrabble or Words With Friends on her iPad. She explains that these outlets offer her the opportunity to unwind. "For me, the only downtime sometimes is on an airplane, and I need that. I just need to rest my brain and engage it, but not with something that's problem-solving in the business sense. There was a point in time when I kind of joked that my reading was *People* magazine." She says you can't be working every minute of your day.

Azalina Adham, the former COO of Bursa Malaysia, struggles to find time for herself. She says, "I go to the gym twice per week and every now and then I enjoy a massage at the spa, but that's about it. Many of my friends go on all girls trips but I don't do that—I don't have the time." The ability to "compartmentalize" enabled Azalina to switch on and off work mode quickly, so she could be fully present at home with her family.

Sometimes it takes a major life event to get us to shift our priorities and evaluate our habits. That was certainly the case for Lori, Executive Vice President and Chief Human Resources Officer at Amgen, whose world was turned upside down when her thirty-seven-year-old sister died suddenly while meeting at work with her manager. She looked at the manager and she said, "I think something's wrong with my heart. I need help." And then she lost consciousness and ultimately died of heart failure.

"She was my middle sister and my very best friend," Lori tells me. "We shared a bedroom growing up. We went to college together. I was her roommate. We got married at the same time. We had our first girls, who are two weeks apart in age. We were very, very close."

Lori says that soon after her sister died, she pulled into the parking lot at Dell and had an epiphany of sorts. "I said to myself, 'I can't believe this is just all there is to my life,' and I quit. I think that was a life-changing event for me. I thought, 'What would happen if I died tomorrow? Is this everything I really want to do and be?'" She decided to take off some time to reassess and figure out what she wanted to do next. Within a few months of leaving Dell, Lori was recruited by Amgen, but the respite gave her time to restore herself.

My mother, Etaba, taught me everything I know about self-care. Even in the worst of times, she could find ways to take care of herself and, in turn, she was able to find the fun in life. This was the woman whose husband got carted away as a political prisoner! But she invested her energy in productivity. I remember her always keeping herself busy with her hands, creating a beautiful environment through gardening and handicrafts. I marvel now to think of how many decorations she made out of seemingly nothing. She was also a master of cooking and derived pleasure from doing so—she would say to me, "If you're cooking for someone you love, it will taste good. If you're cooking because it's a chore, it won't, so don't waste your time."

Etaba found ways to stay positive, even in the worst of times; she always sought the silver lining. One of the most important lessons she imparted to me is that joy is not a destination—it's a daily practice. Creating joy for others made Etaba happy and became one of the ways she took care of herself.

To restore herself, Etaba spent quality time with her lifelong friends with whom she met regularly. They talked about everything and enjoyed themselves. I remember hearing hearty laughter whenever they got together. One evening I saw Etaba and her friends sitting in our dark living room, immersed in conversation. I turned on the light and asked them why they were sitting in the dark. Etaba replied by saying, "I am enjoying the conversation so much, and if I turn on the light, my friends will realize that it is getting late and leave." I always remember this and appreciate how much Etaba valued and enjoyed her friendships. I am sure it helped her forget all her troubles.

But Etaba had another way of caring for herself: time alone. This was challenging for a woman who had ten children to raise and a business to run and who was also a beloved friend and confidant to many. Still, each evening, my mother would disappear into her small garden and have some time to herself, enjoying the beauty and cherishing the solitude. Just watching her, we knew better than to interrupt this benediction. We knew it was a way she restored herself. It was her only time to herself, but it was enough.

TAKEAWAYS

1. Make self-care a priority.

"Health is an everyday conscious decision," points out Bongiwe Ntuli. Find a way to make time for it, even if you are extremely busy. For example, I schedule all my doctor's appointments between January and March. Along with attending to the basics of regular doctor and mental health visits, every woman must also be in touch with other aspects—such as sleep, movement, diet, and grooming—that compose her unique view of self-care and make time for them.

2. Realize that self-care does not have to be expensive.

Time to reflect or play some online games with friends, a walk or run through a park, puttering in the garden, and a long walk alone or with friends are all forms of self-care. Remember that you pay dearly for *not* taking care of yourself, because of the stress and poor health that you incur.

3. Identify your small pleasures and savor them.

Etaba restored herself by sitting in the dark with her friends. Lori Johnston is guided by a philosophy that time can be savored in satisfying bites—sending texts to friends in the morning or calming down from the stimulation of long and hectic days. What restores you?

4. Trust your gut and know what works for you.

What works for your friends or colleagues may not help you feel good—and that's okay! We are all different, and we have to claim our uniqueness if we are going to live our fullest, healthiest lives. Remember, self-care is about pleasing yourself, not necessarily others.

5. Find one or more self-care pursuits that you can do anywhere.

What restores you could be a walk through a quiet neighborhood while you are traveling for business, meditation, a bubble bath, or something else. Until COVID-19 hit, I traveled often for business. It would not be unusual for me to spend an average of 150 nights per year in hotel rooms. One of my favorite ways to unwind, no matter what country or hotel room I'm in, is to drink chamomile tea with honey just before bed. This is my favorite self-care routine, as it helps me relax and shift to a rest mode. It is inexpensive and, most importantly, available wherever I may find myself. I often carry a few tea bags, just in case the hotel does not have any.

6. Find ways to work exercise into your routine.

If your company has a fitness center, use it. If you work from a home office, build in time for a walk or a fitness regimen. Being able to segue easily from work to exercise can make it easier to integrate exercise into your routine. Our lives are complicated enough as it is—it helps when we grab the tools that are already in front of us.

7. Don't feel guilty about wanting to look your best.

For many of us, spending time on our appearance helps us feel more confident on the job and take better care of others. Gerri Mason Hall enjoys the *feeling* of getting her hair done, as well as the results. While making ourselves feel beautiful is perfectly okay, it's important that we embrace a standard of beauty that celebrates *ourselves*, rather than someone else's ideal.

The topic of beauty can be unsettling, especially since the cultural ideal of beauty for decades has been cruelly unreachable for most women, especially women of color. While that is changing—and it's about time!—I'm still seeing many women wrestle with how much they can express their authentic selves through their appearance. Unstated dress codes at some organizations make it very challenging and exhausting, especially for Black women, to fit the standard or the expected image of that organization. Many of us, for example, have embraced our natural curls to express our authenticity, but at a number of workplaces, this is considered "inappropriate." Expressing yourself authentically, such as through your natural curls, can be challenging and uncomfortable—but no matter how hard it is, do it anyway. Looking your best self can be empowering, so go for it... but only if *you* set the ideal, not someone else.

8. Encourage your colleagues and staff to care for themselves.

In her research, Harvard Business School professor Ashley Whillans has found that if employees are given permission by a manager to take time every week to set the priorities in their work lives and their home lives, they report "being 30 to 40 percent more focused on tasks at work, much happier, less stressed, and feel less goal conflict...between work and life demands."[82] This is not only a good reminder for all of us women in executive leadership to take the time to be intentional in deciding our priorities, but also that if we set a good model—for valuing and enacting self-care in our lives—our employees will be empowered to take care of themselves, too, and the entire work environment will improve.

Remember that the vehicle through which you find joy is yourself—which is one of the greatest reasons of all to take care of *you*.

---

82 "Women at Work," *Harvard Business Review*, November 11, 2019, https://hbr.org/podcast/2019/11/how-we-take-care-of-ourselves

Chapter 6

MONEY

"Hoarding money does not make you better; using it for good does."

—**ETABA**

In 1992, Vicki Robin and coauthor Joe Dominguez published a book that was a bestseller for five years, *Your Money or Your Life*.[83] They explored whether people should place money at the center of their lives. They asked us to consider whether, through our work, we are "making a living" or "making a dying" by remaining in stultifying jobs for the sake of money.

To this day, Vicki plays with this trope—whether we are making a living, a dying, or even a killing, i.e., making money to the detriment of the wider community. When put in these stark terms, her concept shows just how closely related the dimension of money is to the six other dimensions we care about. It also shows how easy it is for money to impact those areas for better or worse.

---

83 Vicki Robin and Joe Dominguez, *Your Money or Your Life* (London: Penguin Books, 2008), https://vickirobin.com.

Our attitudes toward money can affect our relationships with loved ones, the amount we invest in our own growth and self-care, and how we honor our deepest values through charitable giving. We must all strive to be comfortable with money, seeing it as a means to an end rather than something that controls us.

Many women have a complicated relationship with money. This is especially true for those who have known poverty or who face the financial pressure of supporting a family. We all need money, but sometimes we need to fight for it. Once we have it, we often have a difficult time knowing how much is enough. Although we know that money doesn't necessarily buy happiness, many of us want to reward ourselves for hard work and provide our loved ones with the "extras," as well as the necessities.

Women start off at a disadvantage: in nearly every phase of our working lives, we are paid less than men. Many of us have had to fight to be paid what we are worth. Women who are supporting others without help from a partner face additional pressures on their wallets. This makes being paid the same as men especially critical. And many times we lose ground when we prioritize family over career.

Along with making money, deciding how to spend it can be laden with emotional baggage. In an ideal world, we would only spend our money on things that reflect our values. But sometimes *how* we spend conflicts with our values and ideals, and the result is a nagging unhappiness.

To have a healthy attitude about money, women must be in touch with their deepest values. Then, they must make intentional choices to pursue an income that reflects their contributions. They must also spend their money in accordance with their values and take charge of their financial security (with help from a financial counselor if they are not confident doing it themselves).

CHALLENGES

This sounds like great advice, but as we all know it is not so easy to pull off. Here's why.

Women's pay is not commensurate with their value.

Keeping women in the workforce, perhaps especially at the highest levels, is good for business. A study conducted by Pepperdine University found that promoting women into the C-suite of Fortune 500 companies strongly correlated with an 18 to 19 percent increase in profitability.[84] Similarly, the Peterson Institute found that a typical firm gets a 15 percent bump in profitability when the C-suite contains 30 percent women.[85] Yet female executives are consistently paid less than men, as PayScale's 2020 "Gender Pay Gap" report shows: executive women on average earn just 69 cents overall for every dollar executive men

---

84 Roy Adler, "Women in the Executive Suite Correlate to High Profits," Pepperdine University, 2003, https://www.semanticscholar.org/paper/Women-in-the-Executive-Suite-Correlate-to-High-Adler-Pepperdine/e5f3025e7aae2ea096f5fe7cc63f-2247183c80de#references.

85 Marcus Noland, Tyler Moran, and Barbara Kotschwar, "Is Gender Diversity Profitable? Evidence from a Global Survey," The Peterson Institute, February 2016, https://www.piie.com/publications/wp/wp16-3.pdf.

make.[86] While the earnings gap narrows when the comparison controls for the exact job, work experience, and education are considered, women are still paid far less at every phase of their career, which adds up to a significant lifetime shortfall.

Mothers are penalized even more.

Working mothers often do not reap the rewards they bring to their companies. Cornell University found that a woman with children is offered on average $11,000 less in annual salary than a woman without children.[87] And the economists Michelle Budig and Paula England found that motherhood results in a 7 percent "penalty" against earnings per child. For example, a woman with three children makes 21 percent less money than a woman without children.[88] While these two reports were published some time ago, this shortfall has still affected the lifetime income of women in their prime-earning years today.

Women of color face additional discrimination and pressures.

A 2017 study by the Institute for Women's Policy Research and the National Domestic Workers Alliance found that more than

86 "The State Of The Gender Pay Gap In 2020," PayScale, 2020, https://www.payscale.com/data/gender-pay-gap.

87 Dan Aloi, "Mothers face disadvantages in getting hired, Cornell study says," Cornell University, August 4, 2005, https://news.cornell.edu/stories/2005/08/mothers-face-disadvantages-getting-hired-study-shows.

88 Michelle J. Budig and Paula England, "The Wage Penalty for Motherhood," *American Sociological Review*, April 2001, https://doi.org/10.2307/2657415.

80 percent of Black mothers are the breadwinners in their household (either as the sole earner or person who contributes at least 40 percent of the household earnings), yet their median pay lags behind that of women of all other racial and ethnic groups by 12 percent.[89] Additional data from this report highlighted the social inequities that impact Black women's ability to earn good livings, such as disparities in school discipline between Black and white girls, the higher likelihood of Black women to suffer serious illnesses, and underrepresentation in political offices. The report noted that the median income of college-educated Black women was $6,000 less than that of similarly educated white women.

An oral history about Black professionals on Wall Street, compiled by Bloomberg Markets and titled "The Only One in the Room," illustrates the painful fallout of being undervalued. "Every single year at Lehman and Barclays, I was grossly underpaid relative to my colleagues," recalled former Lehman Brothers employee Brigette Lumkins. "Grossly, shockingly, eye-poppingly underpaid relative to my peers who were white...When you get underpaid three, four, five years in a row, ten years later that's compounded in your 401(k), in your savings account. I still feel the financial impact in my life right now today. If I had gotten paid just one year what I deserved—that was comparable, I should say, to my peers— then I would be in a very different position."[90]

---

89 Asha DuMonthier, Chandra Childers, and Jessica Milli, "The Status of Black Women in the United States," National Domestic Workers Alliance and Women's Policy Research, 2017, https://www.domesticworkers.org/status-black-women-united-states.

90 Kelsey Butler, "A Banker Says Being Seen as a Diversity Hire Caused Resentment," Bloomberg Markets, August 3, 2020, https://www.bloomberg.com/news/articles/2020-08-03/a-wall-street-banker-says-being-seen-as-a-diversity-hire-caused-resentment?sref=pHsFVc06.

Money is complicated.

Many of us value the quality of our relationships with our partners and our families above all else. It's only natural, then, that money becomes either a divisive wedge or a unifying complement in our interpersonal lives. The women featured in this book showed me how money could be both. These women were most grateful to have money because it enabled them to care for their families. Yet many struggled with whether they were indulging their children too much. Achieving and maintaining wealth that their parents did not enjoy also shaped these women's attitudes about being able to secure their children's futures. But not all of them agreed on the best ways to do that.

The women I interviewed come from a wide array of cultural and class backgrounds. Many grew up in working- and middle-class families, whose members may have their own complicated—even fraught—feelings about money. Few of them have spoken about equating money with happiness or success, even as their careers have yielded rewards and comforts. Every woman I spoke with has achieved financial success as popularly defined: they make a healthy salary, own homes, and are able to save for their future and their family's security.

However, their feelings about the meaning of money vary significantly, and so do the paths they forged to earn their livings. In this chapter, I've highlighted some of the most interesting financial perspectives that my subjects shared. They can be relevant no matter where you are on your journey.

The upshot: our relationship with money is very personal, but we need to arrive at a place where we put it in perspective and make sure we are using it in accordance with our values.

I was born into a financially comfortable home, only to watch my family lose everything overnight when my father was imprisoned. Watching my family have and then lose their wealth in Ethiopia was traumatic, but years later it would help my career because I no longer feared the "what if" of losing money. I had survived it, and it was no longer a big deal to me.

As a result, I've been more willing to take risks in my career because I wasn't afraid of losing everything. I've learned to focus on meaningful work experiences and to treat the money I earned as a byproduct of those experiences. I value success and significance far more than my compensation. By success I mean achieving what I set out to achieve and overcoming the next barrier. In my heart I know that money will come, so it's not as important to me as ensuring I am accomplishing what I want to do. While having money gives me a sense of security, it neither motivates me to work hard nor fulfills me. I'd rather help others grow in their careers and feel financially rewarded.

I also truly believe that when we give more, we get more. We create financial value by sharing our success with others, not only by giving money, but also by sharing what we know and helping people create value for themselves. When we devote time and ideas to helping others grow, we ultimately receive more than if we are stingy.

Mindless saving over time is a tool that keeps finances from becoming a big problem in the future. When I was in my twenties, I read somewhere that the Japanese have a custom of automatically saving 25 percent of their income. Since then, I have tried to adopt a similar mindset. I don't always put aside a full quarter of what I earn, but I always put a certain percentage away.

Around that same time, I also learned the importance of streamlining financial activities. Before then, I measured my worth by the number of credit cards I carried—until an unfortunate incident changed my thinking. I had parked my car on the street and gone for a walk with a friend. To lighten my load, I had left my pocketbook in the glove compartment. When I returned from my walk, I discovered that my car had been broken into and my wallet with my credit cards and a checkbook were stolen. I promptly canceled the credit cards and canceled my checkbook, but kept my account open. However, a few days later, someone mailed back my wallet with everything in it except for the cash. Since the credit cards were canceled, I destroyed them, but I neglected to do the same thing with the checkbook.

The following month out of haste I wrote a few checks to pay bills, forgetting that I had canceled the checkbook. A few days later, I received threatening phone calls from all my creditors since all the checks were returned. That incident really shook me up and forced me to become more mindful of my finances. I paid off all my credit cards, and then I simplified by keeping just one credit card that I paid in full every month. I carried only a car payment and rent or mortgage and whatever utility bills I had. This enabled me to focus on other things. I now live below my means without getting into debt. I respect the value of money, but I don't let it own me.

Lori Johnston, Executive Vice President and Chief Human Resources Officer at Amgen, lives in a financial reality she could not have imagined as a child. Growing up in Texas, Lori started working at the age of fourteen to support her family. Her father worked in construction and struggled with several health issues, not least of all the heart disease that would eventually claim his life. "In construction, if you don't work, you don't get paid," Lori says. "So when I say we were poor, I worked full time when I was in high school. What I love about that time of my life was, I was responsible for helping to pay for the utilities for the family. I was working to make sure our lights stayed on."

In addition to a great sense of responsibility, Lori was inspired by the spirit of her mother. As she says, "My mom still had this joy about her even when she was going through some really difficult hardships. But if you spend time around my mom, she still laughs, she loves people, she loves her God." In fact, some of Lori's financial sensibilities stem from her mother's attitude: she remembers hearing her mother quote a Bible verse from Malachi about how one is blessed to receive goodness in the proportion that they give it.

Just as she had worked throughout high school, Lori also worked to support herself through college, where she earned a psychology degree. And she was not afforded a straightforward path, either. "I'm one of the really small percentage of women with a child who go back to college and actually graduate," says Lori, who was a single mother at that time. "So I've probably had this orientation, or piece inside of me, that I would consider myself a pretty disadvantaged kid growing up."

Once out of college, Lori took a job in Austin, Texas, at what was then an obscure tech startup: Dell Computer. With the success of Dell, Lori's life began to change dramatically. She says, "I feel my heritage has probably been wonderful for me. I didn't grow up with a cent, so the first time I got paid $30,000 I thought I was the richest person in the world. I thought, 'Holy cow, why are they paying me this much money?' I wasn't really focused on following money at all for the first part of my career."

Despite working her way into roles for which she was well-compensated, Lori says her lifestyle did not keep pace with her growing income. She continued to be conservative in her spending.

Interestingly, Lori was not aggressive about negotiating pay, in part due to working in human resources. "I don't ever want to be seen as a CHRO who is feathering my own bed," she says. Still, when deciding whether to change companies, she looked at whether the compensation being offered was worth the sacrifices required, such as relocating and disrupting her daughters' lives.

Her family remains central to most of her career and financial decisions. When she left Amgen to be near her seriously ill father in Texas, she took a position with the Michael and Susan Dell Foundation, which paid a fraction of what she had made at

Amgen. "It was the right thing to do," she says. Who could put a price on the time she was able to spend with her father toward the end of his life?

Giving back is important to Lori, who feels she must pay it forward to honor the people who helped her family when she was growing up poor. "My parents had no money. So from a family perspective, we feel blessed to care for our core and extended family," says Lori. "We give away a healthy percentage of our income and we try to live well within our means and make sure that we're giving back."

On the other end of the experience spectrum is Sylvia Metayer, Chief Growth Officer of Sodexo, who was raised in a family of immense privilege. Sylvia sees how her parents' financial trajectory impacted her own thoughts about money. Her mother's family lost their wealth during the Great Depression. Sylvia says, "There was hunger and there was loss of social status, and there was loss of housing. And so I think that was so traumatizing to her that it basically bled through the generations." Even though the family recouped some of the money and Sylvia grew up in affluence, she says, "I think at the back of my mind, my mother transferred to me her fear that I would die on the street poor and toothless."

Sylvia decided early on that she wanted to do interesting work, but she also wanted to be able to make a living. While most of her family pursued academia, Sylvia longed for a more pragmatic career, something with more financial possibilities. "I don't think I could imagine doing something like suddenly going off with

Doctors Without Borders, because I just would be scared of the financial insecurity." This is what led her to pursue a career in finance and, later, operations and sales, ascending to the C-suite.

Gerri Mason Hall, Chief Diversity and Social Responsibility Officer at Sodexo, remembers not understanding frugality as a child. She says, "I was mean to my mother when I was little because there were things I wanted and she said, 'You can't have that.' I asked her why I had to wear a fake version of what I wanted. I was often pouting because she would choose an imitation and I did not realize she was doing the best she could."

Once she was an adult, Gerri learned that many women (especially Black women), "successful though they may be, are pretty much living paycheck to paycheck because they are not living within their means. They are spending and using their credit cards." While she has been successful herself, Gerri still remembers her parents' struggles and the pain of doing without, and as a result she is financially conservative and focused on saving money.

Gerri says she doesn't have to be "über wealthy," but she cannot be in a position where she's afraid of what may happen. "Security for me is very important," she says. "Having financial security gives me freedom."

Gerri has found that Black women in particular are called upon to provide financial security and support for others in their family, and this creates a challenge. "I think you have to be super careful and honest with yourself," she muses. "What is it that is meaningful for you in those relationships? What are you willing to do when people come at you? There are all kinds of family dynamics. There are those people who will look at you with disdain if you don't give. But you're working hard for that money and they have their hand out—is that person truly in need? If you give today, is it going to solve a problem?"

For her part, Gerri used to always pick up the tab for her nieces and nephews when they were children. But as they grew into adults, she started clearly communicating that when she'd go out with her younger adult relatives, they would be splitting the bill. She's proud of the lessons they've learned as she watches them build their own families and careers. In her immediate family, she admits to spoiling her son. She rests easier knowing that she has created the means that will ensure he is always well cared for.

For women who are ascending the ranks in their careers and earning more money, Gerri recommends they take a lyric from a Billie Holiday song to heart: "God bless the child that's got its own."

Women in committed partnerships are far better off, Gerri believes, if they can ensure they meet their own financial needs. "You do better together, obviously—you can travel the world when you have two incomes," Gerri says. But she worries about young women who can't meet their own financial needs and sacrifice their independence by seeking people to carry their financial burdens. She believes that way of life is simply not sustainable.

Similarly, Lori Johnston appreciates that her husband is "phenomenal with money," and that they have charted a course together that meets their needs. Early in their relationship, her husband initiated a conversation on retirement and savings, and together they came up with financial goals. They prioritized making sure they set aside enough for their daughters to receive high-quality, four-year college degrees. Lori says, "I always told the girls that they will get a four-year degree from somewhere. I don't even care what the degree is, but once you have a degree, no one can take that away from you."

Subha Barry, CEO of Working Mother Media, advises that women not only manage their own money, but also watch over the entire family's financial profile. "I keep very close track of what I spend and what I bring in, and where my investments are," says Subha. She advises women to control their own savings and investment accounts and give input into how the family money is managed. She does not feel that women who earn their wealth should submit to letting someone else manage it.

Another outdated concept, staying out of the workforce "for the good of the children," didn't hold much sway with my subjects either. While they may be out of the home more, they say their income has helped them provide enriching experiences for their children. Still, many admitted that at various points of their career, they had worried that their status as breadwinners might have impacted the quality of their parenting.

After many years in the corporate world, Lori began wondering if she had spent too much time working and not enough time with her daughters. One of her daughters was very involved in sports, and Lori had not been able to attend all her games. When her daughters were young adults, Lori told them she felt guilty for not being home as much and for missing their events, then asked her daughters what they thought. Their answers were reassuring. One daughter responded, "I remember you being at every event that mattered, and I remembered seeing your face...I find you very involved." They both laughed when the daughter added, "Honestly, if you'd been the full-time stay-at-home mother, I don't think we could have been able to stand you. You would have been involved in everything because you're so assertive." Lori's other daughter told her, "I can't imagine you *not* working. Here I want to be a scientist, and look around me, who are my role models? If I didn't have you in the workplace, I wouldn't have a role model."

None of the working mothers I interviewed regretted that having a family may have reduced their earning potential. Rather, they told me some very interesting stories about how they brought their children authentically into their financial circumstances. Azita Shariati, Group CEO of AniCura, remembers being a twenty-year-old student and the mother of a young son. Her husband was also a student, and money was tight. She says, "You can't buy happiness with money. I enjoy nice dinners out, but even back when we could only afford going to McDonald's when my son was two, I was very happy."

Flavia Bittencourt, General Manager of Adidas in Brazil, remembers the first time she brought home a bonus check from her work at a previous company. "I brought my kids to a mall and told them they could each buy one item that they really wanted; the cost didn't matter," she says. "Then we would have dinner at a place of their choice. Although I received the bonus, it did not belong to only me, it belonged to the three of us. I would not have been able to do it if not for their support. Every year after that, they would ask about the bonus!"

Subha Barry, who has adult children, shared that though her goal is to leave her children comfortable financially, she says, "I don't want to give my children so much that they are not motivated for themselves. My husband and I will be leaving the bulk of our net worth to philanthropy."

In fact, many of the women I spoke with have begun planning their legacies and are thinking about how their time and money in later years can have a positive impact. While Sylvia Metayer's career has provided her with plenty of international travel and rich learning experiences, she sees her retirement as her time to make an impact. "I'm able to organize my retirement and the end of my life in a way that has value," she says, "because it's really at the end of your life that you can spend a lot of time focusing on the outside world, because you don't have your children, you don't have your parents." Recently, Sylvia has joined organizations that focus on mental health problems, especially among the homeless.

Like Sylvia, Andi Owen, President and CEO of Herman Miller, sees her success as a platform she can use to give back. She says, "I've always used the time and resources I have to further a cause that's important to me, such as children or animals. Because of where I am today in my career, I now have more resources to make this a better world. It gives me a platform to further causes that I feel strongly about." Hazel-Ann Mayers, former Executive Vice President and Chief Business Ethics and Compliance Officer for CBS, also feels privileged to be able to contribute directly to the communities she is passionate about, including the New York Women's Foundation, her alma mater City College of New York, her church, and organizations that help women of color. "I feel a responsibility to give to the next generation in terms of my time and sharing my experiences," she says.

My biggest takeaway for the treatment of money is this: don't waste it, but don't be too tight with it either. Money is there to be invested, shared, and spent in the right places, not to be squandered or overvalued.

I have come to understand that I am so much more than the money I have. Because of my experiences, I know that losing money isn't the end of the world—it can be made again. That is the mentality necessary to take meaningful risks. Net worth should not be a measure of self-worth or of what a woman has achieved. Professional women especially need to know that money should not be what holds them in a job. Instead, it should be the inspiration to do good work.

TAKEAWAYS

1. Understand the events that shaped your attitudes toward money.

For people who remember poverty in their childhood, or a catastrophic event that ruined their family financially, those memories are imprinted indelibly onto our attitudes toward money.

2. Prioritize building your financial security.

In all phases of your career, make sure you are building something for yourself. Get help from a financial advisor if you need it.

3. Save as much as you can.

Aim for saving a percentage that makes sense.

4. Give some away.

Your money can be the most satisfying when you give it to others or invest it in causes that reflect your purpose and values.

5. Help your loved ones appreciate that money comes from working hard.

Subha Barry points out that while she wants her children to feel comfortable, she doesn't "want to give [them] so much that they are not motivated for themselves."

6. Money should be important to women, but it can't be a shackle.

Professional women need to know that money should not be what keeps them in a job. It's important for women to know they earned the money—but they must also know it did not "make them," and that net worth is not a measure of self-worth.

Chapter 7

PURPOSE

"How can one survive without knowing that there is something greater than oneself? If I thought that I was all alone in this world, I would be afraid to leave my house."

—ETABA

I‌N 2018, B‌LACK P‌ANTHER STAR C‌HADWICK B‌OSEMAN delivered the commencement speech at his alma mater, Howard University. He spoke about the importance of finding one's purpose in life early. A religious man and a gifted and iconic actor, who at age forty-three tragically died of colon cancer on August 28, 2020, Boseman was committed from an early age to fighting portrayals of Black stereotypes in the entertainment industry. As a hungry new actor, he got fired from one of his first roles after he protested that his character—a violent gang member—was too one-dimensional. "Sometimes you need to feel the pain and sting of defeat to activate the real passion and purpose that God predestined inside of you," Boseman told the Howard graduates. "Purpose crosses disciplines. Purpose is an essential element of you. It is the reason you are on the planet at this particular time in history. Your very existence is wrapped up in the things you are here to fulfill. Whatever you choose for a career path, remember that the struggles along the way are meant to shape you for your purpose."[91]

Many of us struggle to find our purpose, and some people never do. But the cost is high. Fame and money are no guarantee for a life of fulfillment. People who are wealthy in power, in money, and in people surrounding them can still die lonely and miserable, while others retire after a lifetime of building a career, only to feel lost with nothing left to strive for.

Many who strive to get to the top measure themselves by yardsticks set by others—money, professional achievement, and other visible symbols of success. Philosophers and religious leaders for hundreds of years have urged men and women to strive for more. So have modern-day business gurus, such as the late Harvard Business School professor Clayton Christensen. The book he coauthored, *How Will You Measure Your Life?*, is an inspirational reminder that business leaders need to strive for something more.

While purpose can be a nebulous topic and one open to interpretation, to me it can be defined as a North Star, a higher calling beyond your own interests and your immediate circle of career and community. It centers you, appeals to your higher self, and guides how you approach the other realms in your life.

---

91 Chadwick Boseman, "Chadwick Boseman's Howard University 2018 Commencement Speech," Howard University, May 14, 2018, https://www.youtube.com/watch?v=RIHZypMyQ2s.

I think it's closely related to the self-care dimension, because it is care of the psyche and the soul. And like play, it elevates us to a place where we can lose ourselves.

Purpose can spring from religion, meditation, or other types of spiritual pursuits. It can come from an experience that shaped us, or a desire to make a difference in a cause that moves us. Or, as in Boseman's case, it can emerge from all of these. Regardless of the source, purpose is how we navigate the other dimensions. In my experience, those who haven't found it must be open to seeking and recognizing it.

WHY WOMEN LEADERS HAVE A GREATER NEED FOR PURPOSE

Having a successful career and a wonderful life outside of work is a great goal. But I believe that women who lack purpose beyond that may be overlooking a source of sustenance and inspiration. They may be facing an even emptier existence than their male counterparts who fail to find purpose when they get to the top.

Why do I believe this? Because women have to overcome many more obstacles than men to get to the top—we have to overcome sexism—and women of color who live in predominantly white societies must work the hardest of all, to overcome racial prejudice and sexism. Because of this, women may be likelier than men to ignore the things that keep them grounded. They may not see that they can work toward making a greater good possible, or they may feel they don't have time for it.

It is easy to use so much of our energy that we lose sight of the things that keep us centered and connected to the world. A 2013 study by UCLA researcher Patricia Greenfield showed that as people become more materially comfortable, they value privacy more and connection less.[92] Another study by Notre Dame researchers found that people who gave away more of their money and their time, and were emotionally available to others around them, were more likely to enjoy excellent health.[93]

Purpose is key to longevity and quality of life.

A study including more than 136,000 participants, published in the journal *Psychosomatic Medicine* in 2016, revealed that having a sense of purpose reduces the risk of dying from cardiovascular events and other factors.[94] The University of Michigan conducted another study of nearly seven thousand older adults. Those who said they had a sense of purpose lived longer.[95] And

---

92 Patricia M. Greenfield, "The Changing Psychology of Culture from 1800 Through 2000," *Psychological Science*, August 7, 2013, https://journals.sagepub.com/doi/abs/10.1177/0956797613479387.

93 Christian Smith and Hilary Davidson, *The Paradox of Generosity* (UK: Oxford University Press, 2014).

94 Randy Cohen, Chirag Bavishi, and Alan Rozanski, "Purpose in Life and Its Relationship to All-Cause Mortality and Cardiovascular Events—A Meta-Analysis," *Psychosomatic Medicine*, February/March 2016, https://journals.lww.com/psychosomaticmedicine/Abstract/2016/02000/Purpose_in_Life_and_Its_Relationship_to_All_Cause.2.aspx.

95 Aliya Alimujiang, et al., "Association Between Life Purpose and Mortality Among US Adults Older Than 50 Years," *JAMA Network Open*, May 24, 2019, *10.1001/jamanetworkopen.2019.4270.*

yet another study, done in 2017, showed that people who say they have a sense of purpose eat better, exercise more regularly, and even floss more often.[96]

Purpose provides a greater sense of peace.

A 2014 University of Illinois study shows the benefits of spirituality to Black women. In the study of more than 160 Black women, 79 percent of them identified themselves as "fairly to very spiritual," a concept that went beyond the practice of a religion and encompassed their beliefs on nature and their sense of purpose in life.[97] Researchers found that the women who were the most spiritual enjoyed better mental health and more satisfaction with their lives.

It's a powerful form of stress management.

Former PepsiCo CEO Indra Nooyi, a devout Hindu, has said that her faith helps her manage the guilt and stress from her busy life. "There are times when the stress is so incredible between office and home, trying to be a wife, mother, daughter-in-law, and corporate executive," she explains. "Then you close your eyes

---

96 Patrick L. Hill, Grant W. Edmonds, and Sarah E. Hampson, "A purposeful lifestyle is a healthful lifestyle: Linking sense of purpose to self-rated health through multiple health behaviors," *Journal of Health Psychology*, September 2019, https://pubmed.ncbi.nlm.nih.gov/28810459.

97 Tamilia D. Reed and Helen A. Neville, "The Influence of Religiosity and Spirituality on Psychological Well-Being Among Black Women," *Journal of Black Psychology*, June 4, 2013, https://journals.sagepub.com/doi/abs/10.1177/0095798413490956.

and think about a temple like Tirupati, and suddenly you feel, 'Hey—I can take on the world.' Hinduism floats around you, and makes you feel somehow invincible."[98]

Purpose can bring us long-term career success.

The late Harvard Business School professor and celebrated management consultant Clayton Christensen decided, when he was a busy Rhodes Scholar at Oxford University, to spend one hour a day praying and contemplating his purpose in life. He said that this contemplation kept him focused, humble, and able to listen to others and ultimately achieve eminence.[99] And a study published in 2016, in the *Journal of Research in Personality*, found that having a sense of purpose through life actually helps people accumulate more wealth.[100]

We feel the satisfaction of making a difference by connecting to purpose.

In some cases, purpose might come from a cause that speaks to us deeply and that we feel transcends our immediate self-in-

---

98 Holly Lebowitz Rossi, "7 CEOs with notably devout religious beliefs," *Fortune*, November 11, 2014, https://fortune.com/2014/11/11/7-ceos-with-notably-devout-religious-beliefs/.

99 Clayton M. Christensen, "How Will You Measure Your Life?" *Harvard Business Review*, July 2010, https://hbr.org/2010/07/how-will-you-measure-your-life.

100 Patrick L. Hill, Nicholas A. Turiano, Daniel K. Mroczek, and Anthony L. Burrow, "The value of a purposeful life: Sense of purpose predicts greater income and net worth," *Journal of Research in Personality*, December 2016, https://www.sciencedirect.com/science/article/abs/pii/S0092656616300836?via%3Dihub.

terest. For example, Ram Charan, a celebrated consultant to CEOs of large corporations, has worked to lift his large extended family in India out of poverty, using a substantial chunk of his earnings. Decades earlier, his family pooled what few resources they had to send Charan to college. The late Dave Thomas, an adopted child who became the founder of the multibillion-dollar fast food chain Wendy's, launched the Dave Thomas Adoption Foundation, which works toward finding loving, permanent homes for children in foster care. Tracey Gray-Walker, CEO of American Veterinary Medical Association (AVMA) Trusts, found purpose as the parent of a child on the autism spectrum and became an advocate for other parents caring for children on the spectrum.

WHY PURPOSE ELUDES US

Despite the good that philanthropy does and the satisfaction it can give us, many of us find purpose one of the most difficult aspects of life to identify, understand, and sustain. Here are some challenges to overcome:

We find it difficult to justify the time.

So many of the women with whom I spoke grew up belonging to an organized religion and attending parochial schools. But as we've entered the corporate world and our lives have become consumed with work and raising our families, spirituality and personal reflection have taken a back seat—we are often too distracted to pray, meditate, or think about how we can be of service to the world. But whether we can make the time to belong to a congregation bears little relevance to our sense of spirituality or purpose. In fact, for some of us, being away from our houses of worship is how we've come to realize that we can discover our higher purpose outside the structure of organized religion.

We maintain an inordinate focus on tangible needs.

People tend to focus on pursuits for which we can appreciate the results, including tending to our families and attaining skills that will help us do our jobs better and earn more money. Pondering our purpose in life may seem a luxury. However, those who've taken the time to identify and practice their purpose say it is a long-term investment in their future. "Had I instead spent that hour each day (at Oxford) learning the latest techniques for mastering the problems of autocorrelation in regression analysis, I would have badly misspent my life," Christensen observed, in a 2010 *Harvard Business Review* article. "I apply the tools of econometrics a few times a year, but I apply my knowledge of the purpose of my life every day. It's the single most useful thing I've ever learned."[101]

The definition of "purpose" is hard to pin down.

It's no coincidence that self-care and purpose are the two dimensions the women I interviewed struggle with the most. These

---

101 Clayton M. Christensen, "How Will You Measure Your Life?" *Harvard Business Review*, July 2010, https://hbr.org/2010/07/how-will-you-measure-your-life.

are probably the least straightforward dimensions—how we define them, pursue them, and measure our progress is highly personal. We can know whether our community dimension is vibrant by how we feel about the relationships in our lives. We certainly know when our career dimension is not working—if we are unsuccessful, that's usually our impetus to change tactics. If we are successful and miserable, then that puts a whole other scope of work in front of us. But we don't have anyone admonishing us or threatening to take away our homes if we fail at finding a higher purpose for ourselves.

It took me a long time to figure out what "purpose" means to me. My own quest began when my mother died in 2001—two days after the September 11 terrorist attacks. I sought to honor her legacy by pursuing an MBA while juggling a career and my family. In 2004, the professor for my final course asked me to write a career-strategy paper that defined my purpose and values. At first, I concentrated on joy and on what I wanted to give back to the world. But over time, and with each revision, my definitions became more soulful, and I felt more true to myself. I discovered that I really wanted to help others and inspire them to achieve their highest potential. I realized over time that focusing on others would make me happy. My highest-priority values became building meaningful relationships with family and friends, creating and sharing happiness, and being kind. These values, and the purpose they have helped shape, are the operating system for how I manage the other dimensions and live my life with intention.

Spirituality is another key driver of my purpose. A spiritual experience does not require a church; one can happen anywhere. For me, one can emerge from a great conversation with a stranger, or from the quiet as you sit on a beach or walk in the rain. Spirituality can be understood only by the individual experiencing it.

I exercise my spirituality through morning meditation and a daily exercise of writing down three things I'm grateful for, three things I'm praying for, and the three most important things I must do that day. I borrowed it from Tony Robbins's 3-3-3 technique. Writing these down creates a more grounded experience and guarantees that my goals, prayers, and priorities are not just fleeting thoughts. At night, I reflect on my day and how I've acted in accordance with each of the seven dimensions. It's a check-in point for me and my surroundings, allowing me to evaluate whether I'm being the person I want to be. Am I someone who honors others? Am I grateful for what's in my life? This also involves taking ownership for what I've been given—time, resources, relationships. For some of the women I talked to, purpose has often included a community component—seeing how we fit into the world at large. And purpose overlaps with self-care in the way that it helps you reconnect with your sense of self while also offering a way to connect with something larger than yourself.

Raja Al Mazrouei, Executive Vice President of FinTech Hive, part of the Dubai International Financial Centre, tells me, "I try to be so many things: mother, daughter, spouse, leader. And I lose sight of myself." She says the book by Eckhart Tolle, *The Power of Now: A Guide to Spiritual Enlightenment*, transformed her way of thinking about control and inspired her to take a moment each day for self-reflection. "Every day I ask myself what I'm going to do for me today," says Raja. "We tend to lose sight of ourselves and the present moment while always thinking of the future, like, 'I will be happy only when...' But what about now? Recognizing that has really helped, and I also meditate daily to help stay with the present moment."

Raja also shares a gratitude-writing practice with her children, where everyone writes down three things they are grateful for and one thing they were happy to achieve that day. "This is powerful for my children and me, and I'm sure they will appreciate this later," she says.

For some women, purpose springs from feelings of connection and commitment to others. "I do think that we all are called on to do more than just exist," says Gerri Mason Hall, Chief Diversity and Social Responsibility Officer for Sodexo. "It goes back to having some impact, and hopefully it's positive. That's what I strive for. I'm not sure that it's [a] higher calling, but it is an absolute calling on humanity," she explains.

Gerri was deeply moved when her company laid off some of her colleagues amid the COVID-19 crisis. She says that one by one they came up to her and told her that despite the sad circumstances her warmth and mentorship had made a difference in their lives. "That is what is most meaningful in the work that I do," she says.

Sometimes purpose springs from a childhood experience that stays with us. Karen Brown, Founder and Managing Director of a diversity consulting firm called Bridge Arrow, remembers when her mother was seriously ill. "I was on break from primary school and outside my childhood home, and my mother was resting inside," she explains. "My cousin was visiting my mother, and they weren't aware that I was just outside, beneath the window. I wasn't eavesdropping; I just happened to be there. I heard my mother talk about how well I'd taken care of her since she became ill, and how it made her feel very special, and how healing emotionally it was for her. That memory is so visceral for me. I wasn't healing my mother's illness, but I knew that I was bringing a healing power to her mind."

"That's when I knew that my role on this earth was to help people," Karen says. "I didn't know in what shape or form. But I knew it was my guiding star, and that I needed to find something that would let me do it."

After starting careers in nursing and dietetics, Karen found a role as Diversity and Inclusion Officer at a large company. At that point, she knew she had found her true calling. "My purpose is to be a voice for the voiceless," Karen says. "I advocate for people behind closed doors, in a boardroom. The fact that I am their voice, advocating for their rights and their equality, is the power of what I do. I'm advocating for access. I'm advocating for equity. I'm advocating for equality. I'm advocating for them to feel like they belong. I'm advocating to make other people understand that they matter." Having a job that is so in harmony with her purpose has made Karen feel at peace. "Every day, I get to do what makes my heart sing," she says. "It's not draining at all. My work is part of who I am, as basic as breathing air."

Like Karen's, Debbie White's values and purpose were forged through childhood adversity. She says her parents raised her to be inclusive and imposed no boundaries about race, color, or ethnicity on her friendships. But when her father took a job in

Papua New Guinea, Debbie, who is white, attended a mixed-race school and was taunted by other white students for befriending students of color. She also would stay with her mixed-race friends in their villages on weekends instead of commuting back to her family home.

"I got called horrible names because I had a broad friendship base, particularly Papua New Guinean," says Debbie, who served as an executive at Sodexo and other firms. "But I didn't buckle under that."

"It built that value of resilience and an open view. I used to say to my mother, 'Each to their own.' That is a very strong component of who I am. It has played out in the workplace...the fact that I do not judge is probably why I built such good teams, because everybody knows I will objectively assess their performance but I'm not going to judge them as people. My childhood in New Guinea shaped this thinking for me."

Other times, people find purpose when life throws them something unexpected and challenging. For Tracey Gray-Walker, CEO of American Veterinary Medical Association (AVMA) Trusts, it was becoming a parent to a son on the autism spectrum more than twenty-five years ago. Tracey vowed to help her son and others like him. She also found solace in Norman Vincent Peale's book *The Power of Positive Thinking*. She and her husband are now actively involved with a group of ninety families of differently abled children.

"In my dreams, my life was always 2.5 kids, the house, the dog, and whatever the accouterments were that came along with that.

But God gave me a different journey, one that caused me to bury the life I dreamt about and accept the life that God had given me, as a parent of a differently abled son who required my undivided attention and commitment to raise him through adulthood," Tracey says. "My purpose is to create the best life I can for my son, and by doing that it's going to also create quality of life for other people living with differently abled skills. These people, in my opinion, are not always given enough thought, whether it's from the politicians, whether it's from society overall. And my purpose is to make certain that I improve their lives to the best of my ability."

Women around the world had to shift their priorities unexpectedly and focus on what really mattered when the COVID-19 crisis hit. During the earlier part of the pandemic, although our offices were closed, I had to travel for work since we were selling the business. I worked from home when I was not traveling. The work was intense, and I needed to be on Zoom or Teams video calls almost all day and well into the evening, which was very draining. I was concerned about our team members and instituted multiple touchpoints at all levels of the organization.

It was hard enough for me to find healthy work and personal routines—and since my daughter was grown and out of the house, my challenges were far smaller than those of people with young children at home. I once had a call with a high-level executive of another company, who was a mother of four young children. She candidly admitted that she was taking the call from her bathroom vanity and shared with those in the meeting that all the rooms in her house were taken by her husband and her homeschooled kids. The bathroom was the only quiet place she could spare. I am sure many others like her were experiencing the same pressure.

For Ma. Victoria Sugapong, Chief Operating Officer at IE Medica, Inc. / MedEthix, Inc., the pandemic encouraged a renewed focus on family and prayer, while she continued to handle her demanding job. "We had an extended lockdown last year, and we saw that as an opportunity to spend more time with the family," she says. "We gravitated toward prayer and attending daily masses, as we sought comfort from the ongoing pandemic. I've been back to work and reporting to the office every day since August of 2020, but our daily routine remains." The experience served to reinforce Ma. Victoria's values and her belief that material possessions are far less important than spirituality and connection.

Some of the women I interviewed spoke of how their sense of purpose and spirituality has evolved over time. Lori Johnston, Executive Vice President and Chief Human Resources Officer of Amgen, grew up in a very religious household and still identifies as Christian. She tells me she attended church with her daughters when they were young, but they have all steered away from organized religion. "Because I've been around the world so much, I've come to see that the aspect of spirituality is very, very different for different people," she says. "Now I have a much broader view of spirituality, whether it comes through prayer, journaling, or meditation. Those things are really important to me."

Lori and her family now live in Southern California in a home that looks out onto the mountains. She says that living so close to nature helps her find spiritual balance. Lori also says that her daughter, "who is really active, would sometimes find me at home. I'd just be sitting in a chair looking outside. And she'd come up to me, and she always tilted her head. She'd look at me and ask, 'What are you doing?' And I said, 'I'm doing nothing,' and she said, 'What do you mean nothing?' And I said, 'I really want to do nothing.' And she said, 'Don't you want to listen to music, read a book? You want to play a game?' I'd be like, 'No, I really want to do nothing.' And I think that doing nothing and quieting your mind is absolutely critical, really important."

As with Lori, Debbie White's Christianity has reinforced her spirituality and sense of purpose, and she feels strongly that she needs to give back to her community despite a busy work schedule. "That is why I am a trustee at a women's health charity," says Debbie. "Because of what my corporate life requires of me, I can't do a lot of giving back, so I've had to choose very selectively. Women's health is very important to me."

Andi Owen, President and CEO of Herman Miller, grew up in an Episcopalian home, where her family was very involved in their church congregation and her father was the church organist. And while Andi tells me she's not a "Bible thumper," she still practices her faith and carries with her the most important spiritual lesson that her parents instilled in her: "It is the belief that we're all neighbors in this world and we should love and be loved. Everyone is welcome and we should help everyone, regardless of our differences."

"It's not about who you do and don't love," she continues. "Our faith, and how we practiced it, was very inclusive and welcoming and helpful. I have this faith that is outside of who I am, and faith in the greater good, in humanity, faith in things that are greater than all of us and that we can aspire to be like. My dad passed away when I was very young, but to me, he was a perfect example of what it meant to be a genuinely good and loving person. And I think that example helped give me a solid foundation."

But does this loving worldview translate into action? Andi believes it does. "It manifests itself in mindfulness and observance of everyone's differences and respect for different views on religion and spirituality and a welcoming attitude. I also think we have responsibility for stewardship and volunteering and giving back to the communities that we live in. As I think about my journey through life, that's how my faith affects me today," she says. "Back in the day, the church served a very different role in our communities, but today there are many ways to build and find community outside of church. I think it's a multifaceted approach; we now have other ways to connect with others."

Consider Maria Boulden, Vice President in the sales consulting practice at the research powerhouse Gartner, and a former leader of the mostly male global sales force at chemical giant DuPont. Maria feels that her purpose in life is to use her considerable gifts to help others. She is not motivated by any single cause or mission, but she has an instinctive desire to help those who have been overlooked. She has taught religious education, run a fundraiser at her church for eighteen years, and gone out of her way to find opportunities on the job and in her personal life for people others have written off.

"God has gifted you with certain skills and attributes and attitudes," she says. "I'm blessed beyond measure in a lot of ways, and I feel like these are the things I have to turn to in making the world a positive place. I don't know what my purpose is, and I don't know if it'll ever actually be revealed to me. But my mission is to take the gifts that God has given me—whether it's public speaking, writing, or something else—and to turn that into something that helps other people."

Maria, though competitive and ambitious, has always put family first. So when her son was born three months early, she asked DuPont for a job that wouldn't require her to travel. She was ready to walk away if DuPont said no, but the company gave her a position working from home as a Six Sigma Master Black Belt focusing on sales effectiveness and top-line growth. The job ultimately defined her career and dramatically changed its trajectory, and yet it gave her the time and space to take care of her baby and her family.

"This tiny little baby completely rippled through my life, not just in a personal way, but in a professional one. And he made it so much better in both dimensions," says Maria, whose son is now a healthy and accomplished adult. "Yeah, I could have poured myself into my work because, frankly, that would have felt a lot better than trying to deal with the emotional aspects of what was happening to me and my family. It was easy to get lost in work. But that's never been the answer for me."

Bongiwe Ntuli, CFO and Executive Director of The Foschini Group, says her sense of purpose comes from prioritizing family and service to others. She says that prayer and self-reflection help her achieve a clear-headed view of life's problems. "I always check how I may have contributed to a setback, accept my responsibility, and then forgive myself and seek to remedy it," she says.

Bongiwe adds that she feels most at peace "when my heart is full of appreciation and joy. I taught myself long ago to forgive immediately." She hopes that at her funeral she'll be remembered for spreading joy, love, and kindness, "but at the same time, [for not] suffer[ing] fools."

For Zhen Wu, Vice President of Legal Services, Asia, for Magna International Inc., a meditation on a memorable poem helps her focus and put her struggles in perspective.

"When I was in primary school, we had a calligraphy post of a Chinese poem in our house, which shaped my beliefs about success," she recalls. "The literal English translation of the poem is 'The fragrance of plum blossom comes from bitter cold, and the edge of sword comes from sharpening,' which basically means 'April showers bring May flowers.' By seeing that poem every day, I took it to heart, and its message became part of my core values. I believed that success did not come easily. I had to go through challenges and difficulties, but they motivated me all along the way."

As these stories demonstrate, purpose is a very personal realm—but those who have found it feel it anchors them and makes them feel at peace.

If you are someone who struggles with purpose, or dismisses it out of hand, your perspective is valid. But because of its potential to positively impact your life and the lives of those around you, it's worth having a clear view of your life's purpose. You must be open to finding it and to recognizing it when it presents itself to you.

I derive purpose from my own spiritual practices, but I'm no mystic. As Thich Nhat Hanh puts it in *The Art of Living*, "Spirituality is not religion. It is a path for us to generate happiness, understanding, and love, so we can live deeply each moment of our life. Having a spiritual dimension in our lives does not mean escaping life or dwelling in a place of bliss outside this world but discovering ways to handle life's difficulties and generate peace, joy, and happiness right where we are, on this beautiful planet."

TAKEAWAYS

Finding your purpose may take time, but here are some places to start:

1. Identify what matters to you.

Having clear values and priorities in my life gives me a true measuring stick for whether I am doing what I want and need to in any given moment. Every morning I reflect on my day and determine my intention, always in the context of my values and my priorities. This gives me clarity on how I want to engage with the world and what I would like to accomplish, which empowers me and infuses my daily interactions with purpose. I am more focused when I review my agenda and think through how I want to approach my day. When I don't do this first thing in the morning, I derail myself and fall victim to my circumstances.

2. Ponder what gives you direction and strength.

Do you have a "higher calling" that motivates you? When you suffered setbacks at work or at home, what inner resource kept you going?

3. Find a pursuit that takes you outside of yourself.

For Lori Johnston, that means staring at the mountains outside her home. For others, it might be prayer or meditation, or immersing themselves in a mission that matters to them. What makes you feel at peace?

4. Make your purpose a priority.

You will encounter barriers—time, skepticism from others, competition from other priorities in your life. But as we've seen, material success is no guarantee of happiness, and identifying and pursuing your purpose is an investment in your long-term happiness and, yes, health.

5. Find a role model.

Andi Owen uses the example of her dad to inform her own moral compass and guide how she approaches relationships. But we are never too old to find someone to look up to. Who do you admire and why? Can you learn something about your own purpose from them?

6. Think about your legacy.

New York Times columnist David Brooks has written about the difference between résumé virtues and eulogy virtues.[102] Résumé virtues are career achievements, money, prestige, and other culturally endorsed measures of success, he points out. But eulogy virtues are your character, your helpfulness to others, and other things that can't be measured. What do you hope people will say at your eulogy? Where do you hope to make a difference, beyond work and family?

Purpose is the North Star to keep you grounded and working toward a greater good. Women, especially women of color, who aspire to be organizational leaders need it more than men. Those who find their purpose will come to wonder how they could ever do without it.

---

102   David Brooks, "The Moral Bucket List," *The New York Times,* April 11, 2015, https://www.nytimes.com/2015/04/12/opinion/sunday/david-brooks-the-moral-bucket-list.html?searchResultPosition=2.

Chapter 8

INTEGRATING THE SEVEN DIMENSIONS

"I have lived my life and made my choices and I am here. Make sure the decisions you make today will take you where you want to be."

—ETABA

Putting the seven dimensions to work day to day, week to week, and year to year will require a dramatic refocusing. This refocusing will not feel natural at first, but with perseverance it can become a system for helping women—especially women of color—live with intention to navigate life and work. Here's a little bit of what it looked like for me.

Although I first explored my purpose and values in 2004 and review them regularly, years into the experiment I was still struggling to make my new, well-balanced life a reality. I was striving to be a good businessperson, mother, and friend, without any clear process or path to achieving this. Four years later, in 2008, I went to the Human Performance Institute, an organization that helps individuals and companies maximize energy and improve well-being. It is known for fueling higher performance and inspiring purposeful living.

Participants in the program were required to conduct a 360-degree review—an analysis of all spheres of our lives—with our colleagues, friends, and family. That was a true test of whether I was really living my life the way I intended. Although my peers' and colleagues' feedback was positive, the feedback from my friends and family was a little brutal. My daughter thought I was working all the time and not paying attention to our family, and she felt I was on the phone too much and not listening well. My friend described me as a workaholic—distracted and not focused on our relationship. This was a rude awakening; four years after exploring my purpose I hadn't made much progress. So, I zoomed in and tried to be more intentional and in sync with my values.

I got closer to living a well-balanced life when I created my priority list. This helped me focus more on family, health, service to others, balance, and excellence. It also helped me make decisions that my 360-degree review had suggested I struggled with. By actively trying to be more decisive and deliberate, I was able to gain a better sense of what I wanted in life: to inspire others and enable them to realize their highest potential. This made me commit to walking the walk!

One of my most significant growth spurts in this arena came in 2018, when I attended an advanced management program. Each participant was paired with a coach to help us define our values and purpose. My coach told me I had the right ideas about purposeful living, but I needed more skills to implement my values. In addition to the priorities I had outlined years earlier, I was able to identify what brings me joy, as well as the values I uphold—relationships, kindness, happiness, balance, and service.

I've refined my purpose over the years, as needed: once in 2008, and more recently in 2018. Each time I had an opportunity to stop and evaluate my opportunities in life. I share these stories to illustrate that defining purpose is a lifelong journey, one that you cannot get wrong. Revising your purpose means asking yourself over and over again, "Am I living the life I am meant to live?" It's about staying curious and open. This is not to say that I have perfected this process, or that I have achieved perfection in all the things I have talked about; my life has had ups and downs. I have good and bad days, but I also have the means to reorient myself when I get lost, and I know I have a place to go to contemplate and evaluate where I am.

Like most things, living an intentional life requires a commitment to finding what works for each of us and what keeps us on course. This is hard work. Many times I was so engulfed by the pressure of everyday life that I neglected some of my seven critical dimensions. When that happened, I would feel "off center." I would often sabotage myself at work and at home and would neglect my health. It took me some time to understand the importance of creating routines that incorporated multiple dimensions and helped me stay on track.

Evaluating where we are in this journey requires revisiting our vision for ourselves regularly and clarifying how we want to show up in all aspects of our lives. I use a 5″ × 7″ notebook to plan my monthly, weekly, and daily activities in alignment with the seven dimensions. Every time I break out a new notebook, I write my purpose, values, and goals for each dimension on the first few pages. This practice keeps them in front of me and allows me to refer to them often as I write my weekly and daily activities. Every day, as I write my actions along the seven dimensions, I look for opportunities to integrate at least two of them into an activity, event, or routine. This may seem like I'm overplanning, and I don't always have something to do in every dimension, but it helps me stay mindful of what's most important to me and how I can structure my day around it.

I like writing by hand because it helps me focus on the task with no digital distractions, but using your desktop, mobile device, or digital calendar is okay, too—whatever helps you keep your priorities front and center.

Despite our best planning, disruptions to our routine can make us veer off course. When I traveled around the world for my job, it was difficult to maintain my focus on the seven dimensions when adjusting to another time zone, or after an overnight trip or several hours on a plane. I learned to be thoughtful about creating an environment that makes me feel at home. For example, I stay in the same brand hotel whenever I can, so I can count on a predictable experience and I don't have to waste time thinking about choosing a place to stay and whether the place can accommodate my needs, and no matter where I go I feel some familiarity and normalcy. This frees up mental bandwidth for me to contemplate more important matters.

By integrating the seven dimensions into your career and your life outside work, you are far more likely to "have it all," though not all at once. Women who aspire to be organizational leaders— or who want to achieve their goals without sacrificing happiness—must make very intentional choices about their careers, growth, self-care, communities, play, money, and purpose. It will not be easy, but it will be worthwhile.

TAKEAWAYS

1. Start with purpose.

Purpose is the North Star that guides our decisions in the other dimensions. A deep understanding of your purpose will not guarantee easy decisions, but it will help ensure that you feel at peace with your choices over time. Purpose has spillover effects that make managing other dimensions easier: it helps us be more disciplined with our careers, manage stress, and take better care of ourselves.

If you can find a way to integrate purpose into your work, so much the better. My purpose includes being of service to others and bringing out the best in myself and others. Through working in companies that are service-oriented, such as Sodexo and ServiceMaster, I've been able to inspire others to believe in themselves and do their best. Karen Brown of Bridge Arrow, who discovered early on that she wanted to be a voice for the voiceless, lives her purpose daily through her job as a diversity-and-inclusion consultant, working with company leaders to ensure that people of color feel like they belong. Aligning your vocation with your values is key to lifelong satisfaction.

"Get your value sets clear from the beginning," says Azalina Adham, former COO at Bursa Malaysia. "Otherwise, you will feel torn apart by trying to please others. Once you have your values figured out, you can feel at peace with your decisions, because they are not the decisions of others but your own decisions. Values keep you centered. While you may not be able to control the environment and events around you, you are in full control of yourself and the choices and decisions you make."

2. Embrace lopsidedness.

Realize that your life will not always feel "in balance." The sense that you are embracing and honoring the seven dimensions over time is more important than living every one of them at every moment.

"I don't necessarily think that balance is an achievable thing, but I believe that integration is what I should strive for, and I know that when I'm away from work I'm going to have to integrate some work into my personal time," says Andi Owen, President and CEO of Herman Miller. "I try to be very organized about my time and commit clear times when I'm going to be with family and when I'm going to be working. It's working pretty well for me, but I will say this is a hard role and it's all consuming. Sometimes I make decisions that are good for the business and sometimes I make decisions that are not, and the same with my family. I try my best."

"Every day, to this day, I make a choice," she continues. "When I travel for work, I'm not going to see my son. I make a choice when I decide to do things with my son instead of working. It's always a battle and a tradeoff. The guilt never goes away, and I've learned to manage it. I know I'm not a perfect mom and I'm not a perfect CEO. However, I think the combination of having both of those influences in my life makes me a better person."

3. Look for opportunities to do things that fulfill several dimensions at once.

You can do this alone or with others. The key to embodying the seven dimensions is to understand that this is not a zero-sum game. Seek pursuits that satisfy two or more dimensions and add to your feeling of happiness and well-being. Along the way on this journey of seeking balance, I learned balance is not about dedicating equal time to each dimension, but about seeing how all seven dimensions interact, ebb and flow. Put simply, I have come to understand that not all things in life are equal. Even among these seven dimensions, we must decide what to prioritize.

It helps if you take the approach of maximizing value from each choice rather than sacrificing something else. When I was traveling to Europe constantly, I figured out how my family members could join me over the weekend whenever possible instead of my coming home. This gave me a way to be with them and gave them some fun new experiences, while I minimized my plane time and the physical wear and tear of long-distance travel. I've also invited my sisters and friends to join me on weekend trips, and I have had many more memorable times exploring new places and doing new things with them than I would have had by myself.

Throughout this book we've seen examples of women who have found ways to improve two or more dimensions with one decision or pursuit. For example, Flavia Bittencourt says that she found that self-care, in particular paying attention to appearance, helps a woman feel more confident on the job, be a better friend, and be smarter in love. Lori Johnston, Executive Vice President and Chief Human Resources Officer at Amgen, sees weekends spent with her community of girlfriends as "one of the best self-care things you can do."

In my experience, carving out the opportunity to have "girl time" with my daughter when she was growing up was one of the best things I could do for both of us. We ice-skated together every week. The rink was forty-five minutes away, so the car ride gave us ninety minutes of quality time and conversation on a Saturday, along with our time on the ice. At first, my daughter, who was in her early teens at the time, wasn't so excited to see her mom learning to skate—she thought it was quite embarrassing. I remember telling her to pretend she didn't know me. Over time, she came to really enjoy those times with me. This experience integrated so many dimensions for me: I spent quality time with my daughter, relished the growth from learning a new skill, and exercised without feeling guilty for being away from my family on a Saturday morning. It also gave my husband some time to himself, which he appreciated.

When I started my book club over ten years ago, bringing together a group of four Ethiopian women who lived nearby, my intention was not only to be enlightened (which integrated growth and even spirituality), but also to find an effortless way to have fun as part of a community. That's four dimensions at once. We cook for one another, rotate from house to house, and discuss the book we've chosen to read for that meeting. Our book discussions, and the time we've spent being present with one another, have led to wonderful conversations and deepened our connection. Something created intentionally brought a lot of unintentional benefits.

Integrating the seven dimensions sometimes means putting aside your instinct to control things. For example, on the anniversary of my parents' death, which is always around Labor Day, I host a weekend-long party at my house, bringing together my friends and entire family to play, eat, drink, and talk. That event ties so many dimensions together. It's the one time when I create a way for the most important people in my life to come together, and it's become a tradition that everyone looks forward to. And it is the one weekend in which I truly put aside all work, focus on my family and friends, and experience pure joy. This is not to say that it's stress-free—a lot of preparation is necessary—but it is so worthwhile. I also make sure that guests feel empowered to do their own thing, which leaves me free to enjoy myself. I make a lot of food available for everyone all weekend, but I'm not worried about creating the perfect environment—that is created by everyone coming together.

As we've seen, living an intentional life means recalibrating and being open to feedback, which may feel unsettling at times but in the long run will infuse our lives with joy.

4. Periodically check in with yourself to refine priorities and make sure you are on track.

This can be challenging. If you have a good career path, you're likely to make money. However, if you don't know how to manage your money, you will be forced to make career choices that meet your financial needs rather than fulfill you. At times earning money will be more or less important than some of the other dimensions. That's natural. But fixating on money and consistently making it the most important part of your life will limit your growth and aspiration. The same is true of your career with respect to community. If you focus on your career too much, you may find you are neglecting your immediate family and friends, and you may lose balance within your community. Once you recalibrate, you might find your community to be a source of strength and support for your career. Your priorities need to grow and change if you want to grow and change, but you need the self-awareness to assess when change is needed.

Finally, along with taking charge of the seven dimensions of well-being, women also need allies in a setting that has had the biggest impact: the workplace. The next chapter explores this in more detail.

Chapter 9

LEADERS AND ALLIES

"Those who respect women earn respectability."

—ETABA

I HOPE BY THIS TIME YOU'RE CONVINCED OF THE VALUE OF nourishing not only a career, but also the relationships, play, personal growth, self-care, financial health, and purpose in your life.

Now you may be wondering, *Sure, I can try to improve what I have direct control over. But how do I deal with everybody else—the people around me at work and at home who may not be convinced, or who don't yet understand?*

This is a valid question. For instance, if you live with a demanding partner, making time for the other dimensions and your career will be a challenge. If you work for a boss who sacrificed everything to gain influence and power in the company, you may not get much sympathy. If your company doesn't yet realize the value of creating an environment that helps employees nurture all parts of themselves, this may make it harder for you.

The truth is that it will be far easier for you to live intentionally and embrace all seven dimensions if three other constituencies rally behind you:

- Supervisors and company leaders who are not only comfortable mentoring, but also actively sponsoring people who don't look like them. This means looking out for their well-being, using a privileged position to identify opportunities that may suit them, and accessing closed networks on their behalf.

- CEOs who champion company policies that encourage and nurture the entire individual, not just the career professional. This should start with redressing the systems that make it especially difficult for women of color to succeed.

- Partners, family members, and significant others who support a woman in her quest to be her best self, both on and off the job.

At the end of the day, you can't control what other people do. But it is still within your power to influence potential allies who are receptive to positive change. My hope for this chapter is that it helps you educate colleagues, bosses, and loved ones about the seven dimensions, find allies who believe in them, and most importantly, help others embrace them when you reach a position of power and influence yourself. So, let's start by examining the roles of supervisors, CEOs, and companies.

CREATING A CLIMATE FOR WOMEN TO SUCCEED

If you are a busy executive, you may be wondering, *Why should I take the trouble to forge a new approach to supporting my employees?* The reason is that bosses have a substantial impact on the outlook, performance, and career progression of their subordinates. Think about your own experiences as you've moved up the ladder yourself. You may remember one or more bosses who believed in you, cared about your personal life, and encouraged you to succeed. You will probably remember being more productive and effective in your work during those times.

That is no surprise. A McKinsey analysis, published in September 2020, found that improving job satisfaction and employee happiness can boost profitability and organizational health. "Relationships with management are the top factor in employees' job satisfaction, which in turn is the second most important determinant of employees' overall well-being," the report concluded, noting that only mental health is more important for overall life satisfaction. The same study found that 75 percent of survey participants said their boss was the most stressful aspect of their job.[103]

In other words, as you've probably experienced firsthand, a boss's management style can make or break a team. With this great responsibility, bosses who truly advocate for women must address

---

103 Tera Allas and Bill Schaninger, "The boss factor: Making the world a better place through workplace relationships," McKinsey & Company, September 22, 2020, https://www.mckinsey.com/business-functions/organization/our-insights/the-boss-factor-making-the-world-a-better-place-through-workplace-relationships.

the fact that women entering the upper levels are regularly excluded from the boys' club through which their male peers network and strategize informally. A study published by the National Bureau of Economic Research found that salary-wise, men benefit from schmoozing with male bosses during sports talk, coffee breaks, and other informal settings—and women suffer because we don't have these interactions. The study's authors, Zoe B. Cullen and Ricardo Perez-Truglia, suggest that managers should try to be more inclusive in creating activities in which everybody can participate. "Are the male managers playing soccer regularly with the male employees? Perhaps you can promote other activities that will engage female employees too," they advised.[104]

Now, if you've ever worked in a male-dominated sphere, maybe you're thinking: easier said than done, right? You would not be alone. A survey of more than 240,000 men and women around the world, conducted by Barbara Annis and John Gray (authors of *Work With Me: The 8 Blind Spots Between Men and Women at Work*), showed that 81 percent of women felt some kind of exclusion at work, while 92 percent of men said they didn't believe they were excluding women.[105] In *Work With Me*, the authors observed that many informal work get-togethers are planned by men and include golf and other activities that men typically engage in—and exclude women from. The authors also reported that men sometimes feel uncomfortable mento-

104 Zoe B. Cullen and Ricardo Perez-Truglia, "The Old Boys' Club: Schmoozing and the Gender Gap," National Bureau of Economic Research, December 2019, Updated September 2020, https://www.nber.org/papers/w26530.

105 Barbara Annis and John Gray, "Are Women Being Excluded?" HuffPost, December 4, 2013, https://www.huffpost.com/entry/are-women-being-excluded_b_4377547.

ring us because they are afraid their actions will be misconstrued and invoke a #MeToo allegation.[106]

The way to move forward from this requires effort from everyone. Due to their proximity, our male allies at work will play an important role. Navigating the post-#MeToo era will require changes in how women and men interact with each other. It need not take fun and banter out of the workplace relationship, but it requires that men view women through a lens of professional respect. Men—especially if they have the power in the business relationship—must have honest conversations with us about what's acceptable, and then respect our boundaries. If you are a woman in power, you can foster these conversations.

The spirit of American innovation has always been defined by the courage to move past one's comfort zone. This is what's needed to help more of us thrive at the highest levels of management as we strive to create greater gender equity. This is not about giving us "special" treatment—that type of talk involves specious arguments about "merit" and other buzzwords used to keep oppressive systems in place. On some level, helping women gain parity with men in the workplace is much simpler than that—or should be. Men need to recognize women's humanity and treat them as they would want to be treated. If men follow this line of thought, they may start to recognize some of the pervasive toxicity in traditional notions of masculinity and organizations. A conscientious man who respects women will model this for his colleagues and call out bad behavior—rooting it out benefits everyone!

---

106 Barbara Annis and John Gray, *Work with Me: The 8 Blind Spots Between Men and Women in Business* (US: St. Martin's Griffin, 2014).

Chances are, you may have a good idea of how game-changing it can be for your happiness and productivity when a boss gets to know you as an individual with unique talents. Ideally, when a boss attempts to understand your seven-dimensional needs, they nurture your trust, give you space, and make you feel seen and heard. This means getting comfortable admitting that your needs may be different. A boss should be curious about people, without being offensive or prying.

Unfortunately, if you're a woman of color, you may often be treated as if you're fulfilling diversity requirements, rather than bringing something to the table. Therefore it's especially important for bosses to recognize each individual's strengths and needs. Bosses must also be aware that women of color suffer an "emotional tax" from the racism, both blatant and subtle, they've experienced in the workplace.

Whether we are bosses or not, all of us must be mindful of all forms of prejudice in the workplace. A February 2018 Catalyst report noted that nearly 60 percent of people of color said they felt constantly on guard to protect against racial and gender bias.[107] A report by Coqual unveiled some of the behaviors that trouble Black professionals the most: not only overt racism, but also small indignities like being described as "articulate" or unwanted touching of their hair. Among Black employees, 65 percent felt they had to work harder than whites to advance,

---

107 Dnika J. Travis and Jennifer Thorpe-Moscon, "Day-to-Day Experiences of Emotional Tax Among Women and Men of Color in the Workplace," Catalyst, February 15, 2018, https://www.catalyst.org/research/day-to-day-experiences-of-emotional-tax-among-women-and-men-of-color-in-the-workplace.

and nearly one in five said they felt someone of their race could not make it to the top at their company.[108]

Bosses, whether women or men, have so much impact on the career and stress level that a woman experiences, so it's important to create an environment where a woman's voice—especially that of a woman of color—is amplified. While the boss's ultimate objective may be to achieve results, productivity comes only from an equitable work environment where morale is high. Think about it as creating an environment where every team member is valued, nurtured, and encouraged to do her best work. The benefit of having so much influence is that you can use it for good.

HOW BOSSES CAN HELP

Bosses, especially men, need to intentionally help women, especially women of color, feel valued. They need to create ways to compensate for the fact that ambitious men already have informal—and largely exclusive—networks and lingo that make it easier for them to be comfortable with and look out for one another. Because most top management ranks have long been male-dominated, men have been able to invest their time in building relationships, imparting wisdom, and sharing important information in spurts—over golf games, informal talk, and after-work drinks. Bosses need to be intentional about creating opportunities for women to be part of this informal system.

---

108 "Being Black in Corporate America," Coqual, 2019, https://coqual.org/wp-content/uploads/2020/09/CoqualBeingBlackinCorporateAmerica090720-1.pdf.

If you've made it to the top, you may have gotten there by neglecting other important realms of your life, as many women featured in this book unfortunately have had to do at times. But now that you're a boss yourself, you have the chance to make it possible for other women to succeed without these sacrifices and encourage them to thrive on the job.

Companywide programs are not enough. The most important contributions bosses can make toward achieving equity include viewing women as multidimensional people with multidimensional needs and helping them work in an environment and situation that allows them to blossom. And, especially if you are an executive or aspire to become one, keep in mind that you're already a role model for other women. Your daily presence models the way people in your company should include others. Your actions show what behavior you encourage and what you won't accept. So create an environment where women can do their best work.

If you are an executive, really get to know women on your team, and don't make assumptions. Every woman's needs are different, so it's important to understand who each woman is, her motivations, her opportunities and challenges, and her plans for personal and professional growth. Encourage her development and have honest conversations. Create a space of trust. Not every employee will align with your approach, but try to get to know your team. The seven dimensions can help bosses think of both men and women as multidimensional beings. Don't pigeonhole a woman in your division as a family woman, or a single woman, or a woman past a certain age. Think of each woman as a person like yourself: someone striving to balance multiple responsibilities, desires, and needs. Let her know you have her back. You would never assume that a man in your division wasn't interested in entering the C-suite just because he had children, would you?

One easy way to get to know female colleagues and/or direct reports is to assume they are every bit as multifaceted and driven as the top-performing men who report to you. In fact, they are likely even more so—they have just had to hide it longer to survive in the corporate structure.

If you are in a supervising position, both you and your male allies should be aware of your bias in how you interact with women; challenge yourself to eliminate it. This takes awareness, and it takes work.

If you ever manage a team that includes women, act as a sponsor and a mentor. While mentorship is passive, sponsorship is active. Mentorship is when someone guides another on how to get information or an introduction. Sponsorship means advocating that someone get a role and providing strong support so she doesn't fail in that role. Otherwise, even if mentorship helps a woman achieve a higher position, she is isolated there.

The experiences of Azita Shariati, Group CEO of AniCura, show the power of having a sponsor who believes in you. In an early post at Partina, the company that eventually became Sodexo, Azita became discouraged on the job because it was not what she expected it to be. She told her supervisor she was quitting.

"That evening, the regional director called me at home and told me she did not understand why I resigned," Azita recalls. "She let me know that the company needed me as an employee and told me to trust her to move me into a different position within a short time frame." The regional director took a keen interest in Azita's development. Both Azita and her sponsor moved up through the ranks at Partina and Sodexo, and ultimately Azita succeeded her sponsor when she retired. Azita would eventually become CEO of Sodexo in Sweden and in that post work to ensure that half of the senior positions in the company were held by women. A Sodexo colleague told Azita that her sponsor had told him years ago that Azita would eventually become CEO. When Azita was recognized as one of Sweden's most powerful businesswomen, she invited her sponsor to be a part of the celebration.

Finally, be a role model—bring your whole self to work. You won't be able to lead your unit in a new direction unless you embody it yourself. Let people get to know your family, your interests, and your values. I'll share a few of my own role models for great bosses here—women and men who've advocated for women and encouraged us to be multifaceted.

Among my many bosses, my role model for a woman supervisor was Debbie White, who regularly brought her children to work at Sodexo.

"I think being an expat gave me a bit of a license to behave differently," she recalls. "I had turned forty, and it was probably a combination of things that allowed me to finally be me at work. So, 'being me' at work means that you can include your family, and you can be open about your values and your perspectives on things, in an appropriate way. I never previously felt empowered to do that because I was always conforming. All of a sudden, I wasn't conforming as much as bringing my whole self to work."

When I worked for Debbie, she was always herself. She talked about all dimensions of her life at work openly, including her successes and struggles. She created an environment that was conducive to everyone bringing their whole self to work. She was tough but empathetic. We need more male bosses like her. I've had the pleasure of knowing and working for a few.

The male supervisor I worked for the longest was Michael Norris of Sodexo. We worked very well together. He loved to debate and explore new ideas, and was always very respectful of others. Even when he disagreed with someone and shared his views and feedback strongly, he made us feel heard. We had very open and honest conversations about race, gender, and other workplace differences. Michael created an environment that nurtured outstanding performance. He has always been a strong supporter and ally of women, so much so that he currently serves as one of only three male board members on the Women Business Collaborative (WBC), an alliance of more than forty-three leading women's organizations.

In my career at Sodexo I have benefitted from mentors as well as sponsors. When the company first started a formal mentorship program, I signed up as a mentee and was fortunate to have as my mentor George Chavel, who was the CEO for North America at the time. George encouraged me to consider lateral moves and take on significant projects that would give me a broader view of the organization. We often discussed strategic challenges that he was facing as a CEO of the region, and he asked for my input. Having me as his mentee also gave him insight into my capabilities, which he leveraged as needed and advocated for me to take on additional responsibilities. I benefited from his mentorship and wise counsel.

Richard Macedonia at Sodexo was an exemplary sponsor. He saw that my result-oriented operations, strategy, and leadership experiences would be great assets in a sales leadership role, even though I had no sales experience and felt I lacked the confidence to lead sales. He saw my potential and encouraged me to make the most of it. Once I took over the sales-leadership role, we doubled the annual revenue capture in three years.

Michel Landel, former Sodexo CEO and Board member, is a role model for being intentional about changing corporate cultures and practices. He understood the importance of letting his employees know that he cared about them—their whole lives and families, not just their work. He demonstrated sponsorship wherever he went. He would correct people who used "guys" to address a group of people and would refer to groups of people as "women and men" instead of "men and women." He made it his goal to form an equitable executive team, comprising 50 percent women.

Along with championing women individually, Michel helped make Sodexo a role model for companies seeking to improve opportunities and work satisfaction for all. In a 2012 INSEAD interview, he said, "In this world, if organizations don't promote and work on more representation from women, they will not be able to meet some of the biggest competitive and societal challenges."[109]

109 "Sodexo CEO Michel Landel on diversity in companies," INSEAD, August 22, 2012, https://www.youtube.com/watch?v=RoF8L6VIZNw.

Michel set clear objectives and measured progress against them. By 2015, Sodexo's studies were finding that their business units where women and men were roughly equally represented were more profitable than those with lower percentages of women. Michel saw the company as a "social elevator" that enabled employees at all levels to ascend. For four straight years, most recently in 2020, Sodexo has been among the top 10 percent of companies in Working Mother Media's Diversity Best Practices Inclusion Index.[110]

It is hard to mention Sodexo's diversity journey without mentioning Rohini Anand, Sodexo's Global Chief Diversity Officer and Senior Vice President of Corporate Responsibility. Michel Landel hired Rohini in 2002 and had her report to him directly. She had unencumbered access to and support from him that enabled her to lead the effort successfully. She was methodical, approachable, and persistent in helping Sodexo become a leader in diversity and inclusion. She worked hard internally and externally to make Sodexo a respectable contender in this space. During her tenure, Sodexo received the coveted Catalyst Award and was recognized by DiversityInc for eleven consecutive years.

I hope by now you see that building good, diverse companies is possible for those who step up and make it happen. If you are in a position of power, you be part of this sea change too.

---

110   Lisa Fraser, "Congratulations to the 2020 DBP Inclusion Index Companies!" Diversity Best Practices, August 18, 2020, https://www.diversitybestpractices.com/congratulations-to-2020-dbp-inclusion-index-companies.

A RECKONING FOR COMPANIES

There are real advantages to making an environment more welcoming to women and, specifically, women of color at the top. If you can launch a career at a company that values employee happiness, you are also likely to enjoy the financial perks that come from working at a company that is making money and thriving in the marketplace. Plenty of evidence shows that companies that value women do better, financially and reputation-wise. If you are in a position of power at a company that has work to do in this area, talking about these potential payoffs with your fellow executives and upper management will make your job easier, and you will all share the bottom line.

A Sodexo survey of 50,000 managers found that teams with a 40 to 60 percent male-to-female ratio delivered 23 percent more gross profit and increased employee engagement by 8 percent and client retention by 9 percent.[111] Happier employees boost revenue and profits, as a 2020 index by Thrive Global, SAP SuccessFactors, Fortune, and Qualtrics shows. The survey of 20,000 employees from more than 900 companies found that those who ranked the highest on factors such as work-life balance, career advancement, mental health, and

---

111 "Press Release: Sodexo recognized as gender balance leader among CAC 40 companies by the Institut du Capitalisme Responsable and Ethics & Boards," Sodexo, July 10, 2019, https://www.sodexo.com/files/live/sites/com-wwd/files/02%20PDF/Press%20Releases/PR_Sodexo_GenderBalanceLeaderAmong-CAC40Companies.pdf.

other factors influencing employee well-being saw their return on equity climb 27.2 percent in the second quarter of 2020, and their stock gains outperformed those of their peers.[112]

Companies with diverse executive teams are also more profitable and innovative. In a 2020 report on diversity and inclusion at 1,000 large companies, McKinsey found that those in the top quartile for gender diversity were 25 percent more likely to have above-average profitability than companies in the lowest quartile, and those in the top quartile for ethnic diversity were 36 percent more likely to outperform the lowest quartile.[113] A Boston Consulting Group study found that companies with above-average diversity on their management teams were more innovative, with nearly half of their revenue coming from products and services launched over the past three years, and thus better able to seize opportunities and adapt to customer demands.[114]

Companies that nurture and encourage women can also attract the best talent in an age when an increasing number of women are getting degrees and becoming more valuable to organiza-

---

112 Lance Lambert, "Corporate America, here's the secret to a better bottom line," Fortune, Thrive Global, SAP SuccessFactors, and Qualtrics, October 2, 2020, https://fortune.com/2020/10/02/corporate-america-heres-the-secret-to-a-better-bottom-line.

113 Sundiatu Dixon-Fyle, Vivian Hunt, Kevin Dolan, and Sara Prince, "Diversity wins: How inclusion matters," McKinsey & Company, May 19, 2020, https://www.mckinsey.com/featured-insights/diversity-and-inclusion/diversity-wins-how-inclusion-matters.

114 Rocío Lorenzo, Nicole Voigt, Miki Tsusaka, Matt Krentz, and Katie Abouzahr, "How Diverse Leadership Teams Boost Innovation," Boston Consulting Institute, January 23, 2018, https://www.bcg.com/publications/2018/how-diverse-leadership-teams-boost-innovation.

tions. Today, 56 percent of college graduates in the United States are women,[115] and more than half of the college-educated workforce are women, according to Pew Research Center.[116] Accomplished, empowered women—especially those newly aware of the importance of nurturing all dimensions of their lives—want more from their employers. Companies that help accomplished women thrive therefore enjoy a competitive advantage.

Diverse companies at which everyone is encouraged to be their best selves will also be better able to connect with an increasingly diverse consumer base. Companies would do well to take an expanded interest in "stakeholders," not just shareholders. Because of social media, consumers are increasingly aware of companies that don't treat employees fairly at work or don't give certain people a chance to be on the inside. In December 2020, Tesla released the results of its first-ever diversity report, which found that just 4 percent of its leadership is Black and just 17 percent is female.[117] That same month NASDAQ pushed the Securities and Exchange Commission to sign off on a plan that would see the elite index push any of its 3,000 companies out of

---

115   Jon Marcus, "The degrees of separation between the genders in college keep growing," *The Washington Post,* October 27, 2019, https://www.washingtonpost.com/local/education/the-degrees-of-separation-between-the-genders-in-college-keeps-growing/2019/10/25/8b2e5094-f2ab-11e9-89eb-ec56cd414732_story.html.

116   Richard Fry, "U.S. women near milestone in the college-educated labor force," Pew Research Center, June 20, 2019, https://www.pewresearch.org/fact-tank/2019/06/20/u-s-women-near-milestone-in-the-college-educated-labor-force.

117   Lora Kolodny, "Tesla publishes its first-ever diversity report revealing leadership is 83% male and 59% white," CNBC, December 5, 2020, https://www.cnbc.com/2020/12/04/tesla-publishes-its-first-diversity-report-here-are-the-key-numbers.html.

its market if they did not have at least two diverse directors.[118] Companies whose reputations are at risk, and that know they need help, may welcome women who can help lead the change.

In a 2019 initiative signed by 181 CEOs, the Business Roundtable redefined its view of the Purpose of the Corporation to go beyond shareholder primacy and encompass stakeholders— including employees, customers, suppliers, and communities. "CEOs work to generate profits and return value to shareholders, but the best-run companies do more. They put the customer first and invest in their employees and communities. In the end, it's the most promising way to build long-term value," said one of the CEOs, Tricia Griffith, President and CEO of Progressive Corporation.[119] In other words, it's become a business imperative to encourage women to be leaders in every organization. It must start with the CEO.

WHAT COMPANIES MUST DO

The ultimate power in any organization lies where the money is made—the operational teams and the CEO. The CEO must be a transformational leader. CEOs must believe that having more women in the C-suite will ensure success in terms of build-

---

118 Michelle Chapman and Stan Choe, "Nasdaq seeks mandatory board diversity for listed companies," AP News, December 1, 2020, https://apnews.com/article/business-board-of-directors-38bceb1f1579518b5b1d97df5b029569?utm_source=morning_brew.

119 "Business Roundtable Redefines the Purpose of a Corporation to Promote 'An Economy That Serves All Americans,'" Business Roundtable, August 19, 2019, https://www.businessroundtable.org/business-roundtable-redefines-the-purpose-of-a-corporation-to-promote-an-economy-that-serves-all-americans.

ing good customer relationships, making money, and creating shareholder value. CEOs will want to create a company and a top management team that reflects the demographics of their customers and the general population. They cannot do this without bringing more women on board.

If you are looking to move up to a job with greater responsibility, you should look closely at whether the company's CEO and board believe that women in top roles help the company be competitive and are committed to creating an environment that helps women thrive. And if you are already a CEO or top manager, you can be a leader and help create this environment yourself.

You might wonder: well, *is* it mainly the CEO's job? Wouldn't the CEO be busy managing the "important" aspects of the company, while someone more like the chief human resources officer (CHRO) should oversee the recruitment of women? To that I would answer: bringing women on board *is precisely* the job for the person who can ensure alignment and buy-in from the other top executives. It is that central to the company. The CEO sets the strategy and has the ultimate say over money. Initiatives that are delegated to human resources executives don't always work out. But once the CEO is convinced, he or she can immediately conduct a review of how the organization is recruiting and retaining women. From there, the CEO can create an environment and culture that allows these women to blossom.

As we've seen, smart CEOs realize that having more women at the top helps a company be more profitable and innovative and connect more deeply with an increasingly diverse consumer base. CEOs also must recognize that women who aspire to be leaders (especially those with families and those who are minorities) face significantly greater challenges in getting to—and staying at—the top of organizations. To help career-oriented women move up in their companies, CEOs and CHROs must help female employees become more intentional about their work and personal lives (in accordance with the seven dimensions), and put in place policies and initiatives that attract more women and increase the chances of their career ascension and success.

If you are a CEO, I urge you to address the needs and challenges of women of color who want to advance and take leadership roles. Simultaneously, from a work culture perspective, you should attack the largest barriers first.

Allowing all employees to nurture the seven dimensions will pay off not only for women of color—who have paid the highest price in their rise to the top—but for everyone in the company. Everyone in the organization must be fully aware of the unique challenges women of color face.

"The intersection of gender and race is too often unseen, and it has left women of color to confront a concrete ceiling," said former Catalyst CEO and President Deborah Gillis, who is white, in a 2018 speech. She pointed out that even white women and Black men enjoy more workplace privileges than Black women, while white men enjoy the most of all. Gillis noted that white men at the top have the most soul-searching to do. "Most of you have never thought about your gender, just as I never thought about my race," she said. "You moved ahead thinking every opportunity was equal and earned; that mentorship and sponsorship for leadership roles was based entirely on merit...You have never had to question whether a leadership position was open to somebody like you; you never had to face the challenge to fit in or stand out. You just naturally belonged."[120]

Such awareness, and the commitment to change, must extend throughout the entire organization, beyond the C-suite. Why? It's not just the number in the C-suite that counts; it's the number in the pipeline. If you're a CEO, maybe 4 percent of all the women at your company are your peers in upper management. But you will never get to know the 56 percent of women who are in entry-level jobs. At most, you might see 9 or 10 percent at each of the levels in between. This is inevitable, and all the more reason to pay attention to filling the roles you don't have daily contact with. You could fill up your immediate team with diverse candidates, but if the numbers aren't there in the levels below, the effort to diversify will fall apart whenever someone leaves.

Leaders need to ensure that women, particularly women of color, are represented and nurtured at all levels of the organization. We must not only pay them well but also care about their lives outside of work. This will help ensure that women at all levels don't get burnt out by an inordinate focus on work performance without organizational support. It will also ensure that if you lose talented executive women of color to other jobs, the women in the levels below them will be ready to step up.

Companies should not only care about employees when they're at work. If you're a CEO, you can cultivate an ideal workplace

120 "2018 Catalyst Awards Dinner: Deborah Gillis," Catalyst, April 3, 2018, https://www.youtube.com/watch?v=DC2IcnmAuYA.

environment by showing concern for employees' lives outside the office. Their productivity depends on their well-being during the sixteen hours of the day they spend outside of work. This isn't about micromanaging or surveilling them. It's about ensuring that they have opportunities for play, time and money management, and connecting with their purpose. Of course, what employees do on their own time is their business, as it should be. But those in the C-suite should be proactive in implementing women-friendly policies and offering services that support all seven dimensions—not only career but also community, play, growth, self-care, money, and most of all, purpose.

Where can the company start? I've observed that the employee assistance programs in most organizations are underused and undervalued. They amount to little more than freebies thrown into benefits packages to make offers look more attractive. They should be reimagined to foster the seven dimensions. For example, why not reward people who use all their vacation time? Right now, most wellness programs I know of seem to be focused on physical health, because the common belief is that this impacts the company's healthcare costs and productivity the most. The definition of "wellness" should be expanded to cover mental and spiritual health, because these factors also directly influence our ability to thrive at work.

If you're a CEO, you can easily expand the scope of wellness programs and other company policies to nurture all aspects of the employees' lives. But what if you are not? You can use whatever influence you have to lobby for them, armed with evidence from other companies and studies that show how well they have worked. You must make the case for them by playing up the business benefits of a more diverse, happy, and well-adjusted staff and citing the impact on company competitiveness and profits—a language most top executives will understand.

Where can a company start? I believe all well-meaning organizations must include a written plan for nurturing women at all levels of the corporation. The framework should include sponsorships, mentoring, training around the seven dimensions, and pay equity—don't forget money is one of the dimensions! I'm not talking about boilerplate forms that only get looked at during annual evaluations. I am talking about leaders investing resources in dynamic materials that recognize the employee as a whole person, such as a review of policies to make sure they foster and shape an employee's well-being and are women-friendly. The seven dimensions can really be the architecture of human resource policies.

Additionally, companies would benefit from implementing advancement and measurement systems that require executives to sponsor someone who is not like them. If you are reading this as a woman of color, perhaps you have noticed that it can be particularly difficult finding sponsors, because people typically want to sponsor people who look like them. I would like to see companies make it mandatory for executives to sponsor women of color, incorporating not only mentoring but also actively watching out for job opportunities for them. Companies succeed best when they give a diverse range of employees what they need to succeed, such as instruction in how to read financial statements, how to create visually appealing and succinct reports, and how to analyze large amounts of data.

It's important that everyone understand upfront how difficult this work can be. This should not be the strategic goal of a single season; it should be a company priority for as long as it takes to get it right. If you are a senior leader at a company, don't underestimate the time and effort it will take to make this happen.

Big structural changes are never easy, and setbacks happen. The process may become less painstaking if we begin with ourselves, and if we commit to supporting the women we engage with every day. Start with the women around you. You can encourage your supervisors and colleagues to be more supportive. And as you move up the ranks, you can help shape a more nurturing environment for women throughout your company.

YOUR SUPPORTERS OUTSIDE OF WORK

So, what does this all mean for you? Do you think you might have room to improve the seven dimensions—your career, yes, but also community, play, growth, self-care, money, and purpose? Where should you begin?

My answer: how about at home?

The importance of having a supportive community—whether a group of close friends, a partnership, or an immediate or extended family—is a topic we as a society must discuss and systematically address. When we first meet our friends and significant others, most of us think with our hearts rather than our heads, without considering whether our values and goals are similar. For women who can envision the life they want to have in all dimensions, and who seek to align their lives with those choices, having relationships that support that vision makes it easier. If you were fortunate enough to choose such people to share your life as friends or partners, you're way ahead. But for most of us, getting alignment from loved ones takes work and some adjusting that does not feel natural at first.

Raja Al Mazrouei's story comes to mind. Raja grew up in Abu Dhabi. When it was time to marry, and suitors for her and her sisters were visiting, Raja chose to match with someone from Dubai. Her assumption at the time was that someone from Dubai would be less conservative and more supportive of a woman who wanted to pursue a career. She made the best choice from the limited options available to her, and her decision landed her in Dubai with a supportive husband and a thriving career.

Debbie White says her husband, Peter, was willing to give up his career and take a supporting role when she relocated to the United States and ensure that the "right family infrastructure" was in place for their sons. "When you do an international assignment, it is a family event; it is not an individual event," she says. "The emotional support from my family has significantly helped my success...including a husband who gave up his career to allow me to pursue mine and also to make sure in times of transition that we had someone home with the boys."

Rachana Panda also appreciates her supportive husband, Bharat. "He always encouraged me even in the darkest moments in my journey and would always talk to me and remind me of the brighter side. I could never have reached where I am today without his support. We have never had stereotypical roles at home."

As you seek to balance your personal and professional lives, one of the most important factors is whether your partner remains supportive of your goals. A 2017 Harvard Business Review article, written by gender consultant and author Avivah Wittenberg-Cox, concludes that having no spouse is better than having an unsupportive one: "It's not that these husbands aren't progressive, supportive spouses. They certainly see themselves that way—as do many of the CEOs and leaders of companies I work with. But they are often caught out by trade-offs they were not expecting. They are happy to have successful, high-earning wives. They applaud and support them—until it starts to interfere with their own careers."[121]

Debbie says she has seen this attitude firsthand. "Something I didn't realize, until I spoke to men, is that it's amazing how many men do not discuss job changes or career changes with their partners."

For many men, especially those who are primary caregivers for children, there's still a stigma that comes with being the less well-paid, more supportive, more domestic spouse. If you are a high-achieving woman with a family and a husband who takes the lead with the kids, you've probably seen this yourself.

I know of one woman whose husband quit his job to care for their children so she could pursue her career. When he accompanied his wife to social gatherings of her colleagues and was asked

---

121 Avivah Wittenberg-Cox, "If You Can't Find a Spouse Who Supports Your Career, Stay Single," *Harvard Business Review*, October 24, 2017, https://hbr.org/2017/10/ if-you-cant-find-a-spouse-who-supports-your-career-stay-single?utm_medium=social&utm_campaign=hbr&utm_source=linkedin.

what he did for work, people didn't know what to say when he told them he was a stay-at-home dad. We need a more expanded definition of manhood. You can start by encouraging the men in your life to be prouder of supporting the women they love and serving as models to others for this.

Satisfying partnerships result when both partners are really fulfilled in all aspects of life. Happy partners are more likely to make sure everybody around them is happy, and they're more centered. That's really where the opportunity is to have a rich life. I've shared this idea with men, and for many of them it's a revelation. I have also frequently heard from men that it is valuable advice they want to give to their daughters.

Partners can best show support by aligning with women around the seven dimensions, and realizing the importance of nurturing them in themselves, too. These dimensions can inform your decisions about career, money, personal growth, and how you raise your family, if you choose to have one. Then you can make intentional choices together—thinking clearly about what is best for you as individuals, a couple, and a family. It will require tradeoffs, and it will not always be easy, but being on the same page will build stronger families. Look for opportunities to do things together that nurture more than one dimension at the same time. Find ways to play together.

For instance, I often work out with my husband, Shif. We also take long walks. In doing so, in addition to being physically active, we address the most challenging conversations about money, relationships, careers, or any other issues. This is a great way to confront issues in a nonthreatening way. I find that when you are walking side by side and having a conversation, the vibe is far more collaborative than sitting across a table and getting serious.

Families and friends also need to be a part of the discussion about a woman's purpose, and part of the team that encourages her to pursue it. They can also give honest feedback.

Conclusion

A CALL TO ACTION

My mother embraced life even when she faced challenging circumstances. She relied on her inner resources to find joy in the bleakest moment of her life, when her husband was imprisoned and she was left responsible for taking care of her large family. My life today is far from what Etaba experienced. However, I not only look for guidance from her in my everyday existence, but also feel responsible for sharing her story and wisdom so women everywhere can draw inspiration from her to live more fully.

I know my mother would have preferred to have a career that fulfilled her, but her circumstances did not allow for that. Yet she made the most of her situation. I have been contemplating how to honor her by living a better and more intentional life. This book is my way of packaging her wisdom so others can benefit from it. It took me some time to get to the seven-dimensions framework, and I hope it provides a simple tool to help you navigate life and work with joy and purpose.

It has been twenty years since my mother passed, and I hope she would be happy with how I lead my life today. She often said that women can have it all if we are intentional, work hard, and enter relationships based on equality and mutual respect. Etaba was adamant about economic independence for women. She used to say that the best way to ensure independence is by having your own income or some way to ensure that you have money.

Though it has been more than one hundred years since the Nineteenth Amendment gave American women the right to vote, the US and many other countries around the world have not made significant progress in creating a workplace designed for women to thrive. Of course, different countries have different women-friendly policies, and a few of us have been able to move up the career ladder, but so much more work must be done. In the meantime, we as women need to find ways to claim our rightful place in businesses and organizations without sacrificing everything else that matters. I hope this book helps you organize your life in a way that honors your unique needs and wants.

In 2021, we are seeing women either ascending to or maintaining the top roles in government, such as US Vice President Kamala Harris and New Zealand Prime Minister Jacinda Ardern. We see women inspiring movements, such as the teenage climate activist Greta Thunberg, and women using their status as entertainers—like actress and talk show host Oprah Winfrey and singer Taylor Swift—to push for social change. But we still have work to do in giving women a place at the table in business. Significant barriers to advancement remain, especially for women of color. Many don't want to make the sacrifices in their relationships, health, growth, and interests required for that small chance at a leadership post.

This has to change—for the sake of women, their loved ones, and their companies. Most of all, for your personal happiness and fulfillment: you deserve to live as a complete individual, not constrained by a stereotypical idea of what a woman should be.

The good news is, it starts with you. We must do the work of determining our own values and purposes, as well as our career trajectories, and make the choices needed to nurture all seven dimensions of our lives. We also need supportive partners, loved ones, and friends who understand the benefits of helping a woman live her fullest life, and who embrace the desire to live a full life for themselves as well. Finally, we need companies and colleagues committed to having leadership that reflects the demographics of the outside world and the full universe of potential customers—and reaping the benefits that will ensue.

Most of all, we need to commit to living a life that creates a dynamic balance, integrating the seven dimensions. It won't be easy: my own transformational journey took me years to figure out, with many stops, starts, and resets along the way. I know some of my friends may smile reading this, since they remember many late-night conversations—over glasses of wine—when I didn't seem to have it all figured out. We'd debate whether my new approach was practical, and whether it was possible to bring everyone else in our lives along on this journey. Although it took me many years to get to the point where I could turn what I've learned into a book, I have benefited from this approach along the way. I know that with the help of this seven-dimensional framework, your journey won't take as long.

Creating a workplace that encourages women to bring their whole selves to work is good for everyone. Also, the seven dimensions are not for women only. Remember to share your wealth of knowledge with the men in your lives, too, including your partner and coworkers. Better yet, encourage them to read this book. They will likely enjoy more fulfillment and happier lives as they progress up the career ladder if they pay attention to creating a dynamic balance of the seven dimensions. I'm confident from my own experience, and those of many strong women in this book, that if you aspire to realize your potential both in the workplace and at home, you are already leading by example. Many men and women, just by knowing you, will follow suit. As this happens, we can all look forward to a future in which it will be far easier for all of us to lead more productive and happier lives.

As I learned from Etaba, we are so much more than the sum of our accomplishments, our material wealth, and our influence. Living with intention—and honoring our need for community, play, growth, self-care, money, and purpose, as well as a career— will help us feel both joyful and serene and create a world that is better for everyone.

ACKNOWLEDGMENTS

This book would not be possible without my true inspirations: my parents, who made my existence possible, especially my mother, for her incredible wisdom and for being the most amazing mother...and to my one-of-a-kind father who I can still remember challenging me to stretch out of my comfort zone when he asked me to write an essay in third grade and encouraged me to read it to everyone at the dinner table. Although I only got to spend a small part of my life with him, he left an indelible mark in my life and is the reason for the confidence I possess today. He always made me feel I could do anything. I am grateful to him for spending so much time with us and driving his children to school and back every day. Even though I lost my parents nearly twenty years ago within a period of eleven months of each other, I continue to draw inspiration from them every day.

My primary gratitude goes to Shif, my husband, for encouraging me in all possible ways to build my career and to write this book. He was often the first to review each chapter and each version and let me know what needed more work or when I was almost there. His absolute drive for quality and his belief that the book could be even better throughout the process inspired me to try harder and dig deeper. I am also so grateful for my daughter,

Helen. Her persistence for excellence has been an inspiration to me. I try to emulate her kindness, strength, and stamina. Helen did not know my mother, Etaba, since Helen was only five years old when Etaba passed. By reading this book, I hope Helen will get a glimpse into her grandmother's strength and wisdom.

To all my siblings, who in some ways contributed to who I am today and for listening to me blather about everything, especially this book. I am forever grateful. I will always be thankful to DeeDee for her sacrifice, guidance, and support. I am always in awe of her optimism and can-do attitude. If I could define and package kindness in one person, it would be in my sister Tigest. Her selflessness in every way inspires me to be a little kinder. My sister Beli can easily be called my therapist. She is one of those people with whom I have always been able to share in confidence my thoughts, ideas, and complaints, knowing she always gives sage advice and is never shocked by whatever she hears. To a truly fantastic human being, my brother Sami/Anberber, who I call for anything I need and know he will answer his phone with a smile and make me feel I did not interrupt him, even if it is in the middle of the night. For a brother who taught me not to be afraid of the dark, Daniel. He only lived in this world a short twenty years when he sacrificed himself fighting for what he believed in. He was a serious soul who came into this world to inspire us all with his courage, brain power, and determination. For my best friend for as long as I remember, my brother, Naod, I don't know a day that I have not talked to him. He has always protected me as his younger sister and tried to include me in his boys' clubs and ensured that my voice mattered. If wisdom and storytelling ability are given at birth, Minilik received plenty of it. I am in awe of his smarts, and I never get tired of listening to him. He always reminded me of my higher calling and assured me that "even this will pass." I love and respect my brother Agidew's quiet presence; he has a way of being heard without saying a word. I appreciate and thank him for being there for Etaba; I know she counted on him. To Mamush/Wondwosen: although he is my baby brother, I feel we are like twins in so many ways. We have so much in common, and I think he is a male version of me.

I want to express my immense gratitude to all those who read all or sections of this book and provided feedback: Shif Berhanu, DeeDee Angagaw, Merafe Tesfaye, Rebecca Hailu, Ejigayehu Demissie, Elizabeth Allman, and Diane Galutia. I would also like to thank Bayeh Tesfaye for his expert support.

Most of all, I am indebted to all the women in this book who gave their time and shared their stories freely. This book would not be possible without their stories.

I would like to thank the talented team who supported me in bringing this book to life. I especially would like to express my gratitude to Cathy Buday and Bob Buday, who provided expert guidance and help in structuring the book and enhancing the research; to Abigail Santamaria, Kera Bolonik, and Holly Van Leuven, for their contribution in the development of the manuscript and initial editing; and Diane Galutia for her ongoing support. From the publishing team, I would like to thank Katie Villalobos for excellent project management and getting the book to print on time; to Anna Dorfman for her brilliant cover design and the many iterations she created so quickly; to Charity Young for the excellent final editing of the manuscript; and to all those who helped in any way.

I want to acknowledge my amazing and fiercely independent mother-in-law, Yemisrach Haile, who passed away as I was finishing this book. She was an epitome of an independent woman who often went against tradition for what is fair and just. She was a great example and inspiration to her kids, to me, and to all those who knew her. She will be missed.

ABOUT THE AUTHOR

Aster Angagaw is the seventh of ten children, born and raised in Ethiopia during a time when her parents faced tremendous struggles. In the face of many challenges, her mother, whom her children lovingly called Etaba (meaning "big sister"), was the glue that held the family together. Aster shares Etaba's profound wisdom throughout this book.

Through hard work and her mother's inspiration, Aster continued her lifelong journey for growth, earned a BA in organizational management from Eastern University and an executive MBA from Temple University, and became a graduate of the Harvard University Advanced Management Program. Today, she has more than twenty-five years of senior leadership experience in global multibillion-dollar corporations.

Printed in Great Britain
by Amazon

84325430R00144